A City That Sings

A City That Sings

Cincinnati's Choral Tradition
1800—2012

CATHERINE ROMA, EDITOR

Orange *frazer* Press
Wilmington, Ohio

ISBN 978-1933197-913
Copyright©2012 May Festival

Published for Cincinnati Musical Festival Association by:
Orange Frazer Press
P.O. Box 214
Wilmington, OH 45177
Telephone: 800.852.9332 for price and shipping information.
Website: www.orangefrazer.com
www.orangefrazercustombooks.com

Cincinnati Musical Festival Association
Music Hall
1241 Elm Street
Cincinnati, Ohio 45202
www.mayfestival.com
513.621.1919

Copy editor: Karin Pendle
Text preparation: Mark Palkovic
Book and cover design: Brittany Lament, Orange Frazer Press
Photographs of Music Hall courtesy of Robert Flischel:
front cover, end sheets, icon on title page, pgs. 120-121, 234-235

Library of Congress Control Number 2011945962

Printed in China

DEDICATION

To the thousands of Cincinnatians of all musical and ethnic backgrounds who have raised their voices in song over the past two centuries to create the rich tradition detailed in the following pages.

TABLE OF CONTENTS

ACKNOWLEDGMENTS

No one completes a project like this one without owing thanks to many people and institutions who contributed suggestions and materials to the work. I thank the staffs of the University of Cincinnati's Archives and Rare Books Library, the Cincinnati Historical Society, and the Public Library of Cincinnati and Hamilton County for helping me to locate research materials and illustrations for my chapter. I am especially grateful to Cynthia Perin Annett, great-granddaughter of Louis Aiken and great-great-granddaughter of Charles Aiken, for sending me information on her illustrious family of music educators and allowing me to reproduce their portraits in my chapter. To Earl Rivers, Tom Merrill, Randy Pennington, Christopher Eanes, Lisa Peters, David Bell, Rick Hand, and Robyn Lana I owe many thanks for information about and photos of the groups and programs which have been their charges. Finally, a giant-sized thank you to my husband Frank Pendle for assistance in research, photography, and all the other things that go into making a pile of facts into a manuscript.

—*Karin Pendle*

There are many people who worked behind the scenes to make this project possible. The other contributors to this book—Drs. Karin and Frank Pendle and Dr. Catherine Roma—turned an idea into reality. Special thanks go to Karin for her eagle eye and Cathy for her unswerving belief in this project. Steven Sunderman and the Cincinnati May Festival deserve accolades for their generous support of this project. Other notables are: Don Heinrich Tolzmann, the eminent authority on the Germans of Cincinnati, for his insight and enthusiasm; Linda Bailey of the Cincinnati Historical Society Library for her help in finding the magnificent photographs; and the World Choir Games for initiating the project. But most of all, I am grateful to James Dreigon for giving daily support through his historical knowledge and personal encouragement throughout the two years leading to publication.

—*Craig Doolin*

My chapter would not have been possible were it not for many generous people who took the time to be interviewed, read initial drafts of the work, or donated files of programs and pictures. I met with individuals in church basements, beautiful homes across the city, downtown restaurants, and local archival repositories. The following people helped me develop a picture of Cincinnati's African American music community. Their encouragement and support motivated me as I sprinted toward the finish line. I express my deepest gratitude for the willingness of people who came forward, on short notice, to make this chapter a reality. To my mentors who continue to exert an everlasting influence, to old and newfound friends who supported and guided me, to the people I interviewed who joyfully remembered formative musical experiences that marked their lives, thank you. Special mention goes to Ysaye Maria Barnwell, Craig Doolin, Janelle Gelfand, Greta Gibson, Tammy Kernodle,

Andrea Tuttle Kornbluh, Eric V. Oliver, Karin
Pendle, Bernice Johnson Reagon, Daphne
Robinson, and those interviewed listed here:
M. Ruth Brown Phillips, John Bailey, Johanna
Byrd, Louisa Dickey, Robert Gazaway, Ann
Greene, Herbert Mitchell, Glondora Moore,
Eric V. Oliver, Daphne Robinson, Irma Tillery,
Sherrie Turner. Special thanks to the following
librarians: Jean Mulhern, Director of Watson
Library, Wilmington College; Patti Kinsinger,
Head of Reference Department, Wilmington
College; Linda J. Bailey, Curator of Prints and
Photographs, Cincinnati Historical Society;
Andy Balterman and Chris Smith of The Public
Library of Cincinnati and Hamilton Co.; Mark
Palkovic, Head Librarian, College-Conservatory
Music Library, University of Cincinnati; and
Kevin Grace, Head of Archives and Rare
Book Library, University of Cincinnati. Wynn
Alexander, Nathan Bachrach, Michael Black,
Barbara Bouldin, Verneida Britton, Lillie Brown,
John Bryant, William Caldwell, Althea Day,
Ruth Dobyns, Christine Engles, Eugenia Ewing,
Kathy Finley, Elizabeth Haskins, Rachel Kramer,
Lori Lobsiger, Charmaine Moore, Bishop Todd
O'Neal, Jim Reynolds, David Sandor, Amanda
Schear, Betty J. Smith, Dorothy Smith, Steven
Sunderman, Nikki M. Taylor, Rosanne Wetzel,
Tracy Wilson. Earl Rivers, Artistic Director; M.
Kim Mann, who co-chaired with me, Christopher
Eanes, Kanniks Kannikeswaren, Rachel Kramer,
and Robyn Lana. INTERKULTUR World Choir
Games USA 2012: Piroska Horvath, Stefan
Bohlander, Wolfgang Coym, Jelena Dannhauer,
Gent Lazri, Lori Lobsiger, M. Kim Mann, Stefan
Piendl, Matthias Timmlau.

—*Catherine Roma*

FOREWORD

The City of Cincinnati proudly hosts the World Choir Games Cincinnati 2012, the first World Choir Games held in the USA. *A City That Sings: Cincinnati's Choral Tradition 1800-2012* celebrates this significant international choral event by illuminating the rich choral legacy of the Queen City. Reading *A City That Sings*, one could believe that the USA's choral epicenter is snugly centered in Ohio's southwestern corner.

Cincinnati in 2012 boasts not one, but two nationally recognized children's multi-choir organizations (Cincinnati Boychoir and Cincinnati Children's Choir), the oldest continuing choral festival in the Western Hemisphere (May Festival), an acclaimed professional chamber choir (Cincinnati's Vocal Arts Ensemble), national award-winning female and male barbershop ensembles (Cincinnati Sound Chorus and Southern Gateway Chorus), notable church, community, school, and university choruses (Xavier University), and internationally recognized choral and graduate choral conducting programs (University of Cincinnati College-Conservatory of Music). These groups serve as testaments to the artistry and vitality of choral music in the greater Cincinnati community. Cincinnati also has a rich heritage of African American choirs, both in churches and concert halls, and LGBT-inclusive choruses (MUSE Cincinnati's Women's Choir and Cincinnati Men's Chorus) that have also shaped choral culture in the Queen City.

The three major choral service organizations in the United States selected Cincinnati in the past decade for conferences, conducting training master classes, workshops and board meetings: ACDA (American Choral Directors Association), Chorus America, and NCCO (National Collegiate Choral Organization), clearly affirming Cincinnati's national choral presence. Finally, Chorus America's Choral Impact Study 2009 documented the importance of choral singing in the USA:

"Choral singing continues to be the most popular form of participation in the performing arts, with 18.1% of households reporting one or more adults currently participating in a chorus, and when children are added to the equation, participation jumps to 22.9% of households. When the total number of choral singers per household are tallied, there are an estimated 32.5 million adults regularly singing in choruses today and 42.6 million Americans overall (including children)"

Documenting over two centuries of vibrant choral activity in Cincinnati, from the time of Haydn's *The Creation* (1798) to the creative new choral works being composed today, *A City That Sings: Cincinnati's Choral Tradition 1800-2012* shows that choral singing in Cincinnati has been, and continues to be, the most popular form of participation in the performing arts in Cincinnati.

—*Earl Rivers*
Artistic Director USA,
World Choir Games Cincinnati 2012.
Professor of Music and
Director of Choral Studies,
College-Conservatory of Music,
University of Cincinnati.
Music Director Emeritus,
Cincinnati's Vocal Arts Ensemble.

PREFACE

A City That Sings: Cincinnati's Choral Tradition, 1800-2012 highlights and honors the rich history of this city's choral arts. Inspired by the choice of Cincinnati to host the World Choir Games 2012, this book has been a collaborative project of the Cincinnati Music Advisory Committee for World Choir Games 2012.

Upon hearing that the World Choir Games had chosen Cincinnati as the site of their seventh international festival, I thought—as did many others—that this was exciting news for our city, but I wondered how Cincinnati managed to rise to the top when nearly twenty cities worldwide were competing for this honor. Since 2000 the biennial World Choir Games have been held only in Europe or Asia, never in North America.

The complete story of how Cincinnati became the first city in the United States to host the Games may never be known. However, there is little doubt that the original seed was planted by the late Cincinnati Pops conductor Erich Kunzel. His vision and foresight cannot be overstated. He wished the world to know Cincinnati as one of music's world-class cities, with its May Festival, Cincinnati Symphony Orchestra, Cincinnati Pops, and Cincinnati Opera, as well as its diverse community organizations and its internationally regarded music school. This book and the Seventh World Choir Games 2012 are testaments to his dream and initiative.

Behind the scenes Venus Kent, of the Cincinnati USA Convention and Visitors Bureau, lost no time following up on Kunzel's lead to secure the Games for Cincinnati. The Choir Games were founded by INTERKULTUR, with the purpose of uniting people of all ages and nations through choral music. Their motto is: "Singing together brings nations together." Gunter Titsch, the President of Interkultur, and artistic directors Ralf Eisenbeiß (Germany), Gabor Hollerung (Hungary), and Christian Ljunggren (Sweden) visited Cincinnati frequently, met with our Music Advisory Committee, listened to area choral groups, and evaluated many viable performance halls and auditoriums. They concluded:

"Great beauty and great sound is abundant in Cincinnati theatres, concert halls, and churches. This is truly a grand city for singing."

Not only had the venues captivated them, but the passion for singing and the choral heritage of the nineteenth-century Saengerfest remained in the fiber of Cincinnati's musical community.

Each of the authors contributing to this book brings specific expertise and insights to this history. In Chapter One, "Becoming the Queen City: An Overview," historian Frank Pendle provides an overview of Cincinnati, tracing the developments in her growth through commerce, government, education, and the arts. This sketch illustrates the shifting social and cultural landscapes in Cincinnati out of which the thriving choral music scene emerged.

In "Queen City of Song: Choral Music in Cincinnati Schools, Conservatories, and Universities," musicologist Karin Pendle highlights the cultivation of a robust choral curriculum and commitment to music education from the earliest schools in the nineteenth century through the strong emphasis on choral music in Cincinnati's institutions of higher learning in the twentieth century. Reading of the advances and the importance of singing in the city's public, parochial, and "colored" schools, one begins to understand how the institutions and singing societies developed with capable, musically literate choristers. This formidable singing tradition continues unabated into the twenty-first century, and area schools and colleges are highlighted.

In Chapter Three, "Singing Schools, Social Music, and Choral Festivals," musicologist Craig Doolin stresses Cincinnati's tradition of singing societies as an important foundation of choral music in the Queen City. He identifies the importance of both the English and the German traditions as basic to the founding of the May Festival, with its unique mixture of repertoire and performing forces. These independent choral organizations and societies continue to thrive in Cincinnati today.

In Chapter Four, "Cincinnati's African American Choral Tradition," choral conductor Catherine Roma traces the history of ensemble singing in the city's African American community. From churches in the early nineteenth century to the development of independent institutions founded by African American musicians in the twentieth century, they were determined to create autonomous spaces in their segregated city, where they could develop their abilities through strong music education and choral organizations.

From varied vantage points the authors offer a glimpse into the rich past and ongoing passion for choral music in Cincinnati. Choral communities continue to bring diverse people together. Over the last thirty years especially, professional and amateur singers from different backgrounds, neighborhoods, and faith traditions continue to prove the power of the choral arts to transcend differences and unite communities.

—*Catherine Roma*
Professor of Music,
Wilmington College.
Founder and Director,
MUSE, Cincinnati's Women's Choir.
Minister of Music at St. John's
Unitarian Universalist Church.
Co-Founder and Co-Director,
Martin Luther King Chorale.
Founder and Director,
UMOJA Men's Chorus,
Warren Correctional Institution.

A City That Sings

Becoming
THE QUEEN CITY:
An Overview

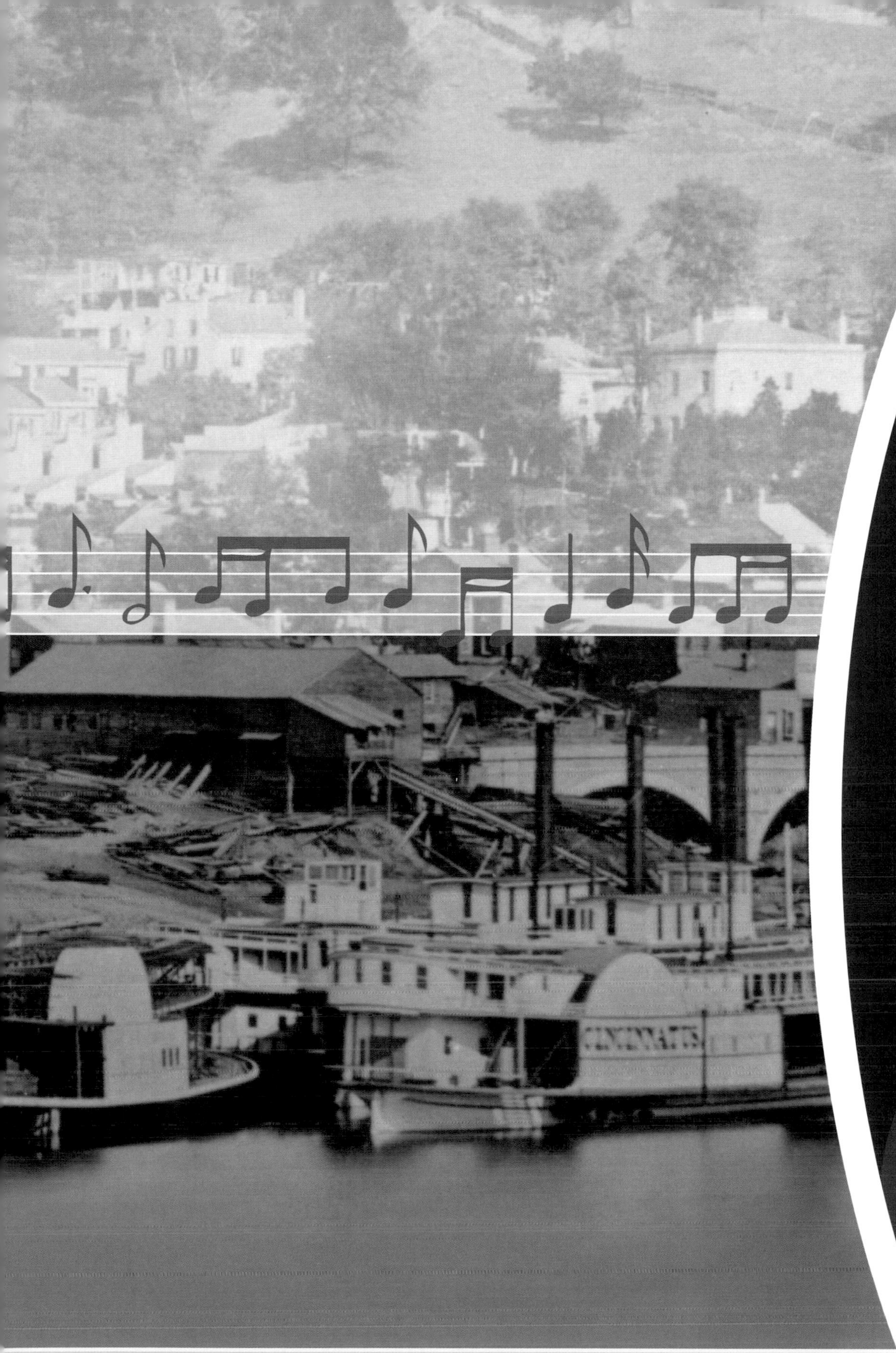

Chapter One

by Frank Pendle

Fort Washington Garrison, 1789-1809, on the Ohio River at the site of Losantiville (later, Cincinnati). The fort housed up to 300 soldiers. Oil painting by C. A. Wiltsee. (Courtesy of Cincinnati Historical Society)

Cincinnati is a community of nearly 300,000, set within an urban area of about 1.5 million that stretches across and back from the mighty Ohio River. In fact, this river, which forms the southern boundary of the states of Ohio, Indiana, and Illinois, and the northern boundary of Kentucky, is the primary reason that the seeds that grew into the city of Cincinnati were planted, in 1788, to develop into the present-day urban community. The river was an all-purpose natural resource, and became the road by which new settlers arrived from the East or left to seek opportunities further in the West. Household goods followed on flat-bottom boats propelled by river currents and oarsmen to their new homes in the bustling village that would be Cincinnati.

As manufacturing and food-processing businesses developed, drawing on the resources of the surrounding countryside, the boats channelled their products from Cincinnati's riverfront docks to distant trading centers. Water, in the form of canals as well as such nearby streams as the Little and Great Miami Rivers, the Scioto River, and Kentucky's Licking River, enlarged the potential settlement and trading area of which

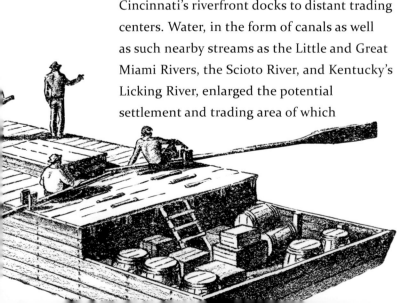

Cincinnati was the increasingly strong and prosperous center. The Miami and Erie Canal, opened in 1827, gave the city's industries access to the land and people to the North. Some would see the growth of railroads as a future threat to this water-based trade network. Others believed that railroads would surely have their uses, but that was long in the future. Meanwhile, the Ohio River was a God-given resource, and it was free. To the east of this active center of commerce, the soldiers of Fort Washington kept the new city's residents safe and even provided occasional musical and dramatic entertainments.

The rich agricultural lands that surrounded Cincinnati became the basis for a lively trade in corn meal and flour, ground in the city's busy grist mills, along with flaxseed oil, corn whiskey, and the cotton and woolen fabrics that were promptly made into clothing for export to the rest of the country. By the 1850s the value of Cincinnati-made clothing had risen to nearly $15 million. Corn fed the hundreds of hogs that were being processed in Cincinnati plants: some 600,000 animals by 1861, when the beginning of the Civil War cut into this and other agriculture-based ventures. At the same time, Cincinnati became home to the second largest iron works in what was then the American West, and was nearly

The Miami and Erie Canal, bordering Cincinnati's Over-the-Rhine district, opened in 1827 and closed in segments by 1910. (Courtesy of Cincinnati Historical Society)

the equal of Pittsburgh in the production of steamboats. Trees from nearby forests provided materials for fine furniture and lumber to be shipped out for construction projects further south or west. Alongside these manufactories came banks, insurance companies, investment brokerages, law offices, and the rest of the supporting cast that backed the city's prosperity. By 1850 Cincinnati was America's sixth largest city and ranked third as a producer of manufactured goods of great variety and respected quality, distributed largely through the network of rivers and canals that connected the city with the rest of the country. According to the 1860 census Cincinnati's population had risen to 161,000, and its position as the foremost producer of goods and the social leader in the area earned it the appellation "Queen City of the West."

CINCINNATI'S GROWING PAINS

At the base of Cincinnati's growth stood an initial group of settlers: native-born Americans of English or Scotch-Irish origins. After 1830 came the first wave of German immigrants, bringing with them the beer halls and singing societies that still seem basic to the character of the city. Jewish Germans, led by Rabbi Isaac M. Wise and Max Lilienthal, established Reform Judaism in America and opened Hebrew Union College in 1876 to educate future rabbis and other essential leaders in the Jewish community. Jews from other European countries joined what became, by the mid-19th century, the third Jewish community in America, the oldest such community west of the Alleghenies.

Boats are moored at Public Landing (now The Banks) in "View of Cincinnati from Covington, Kentucky" by John Caspar Wild (1835). Gouache on paper. (Courtesy of Cincinnati Historical Society)

The potato famines of the 1840s caused many Irish to leave their homeland to resettle in Cincinnati and other cities of America. Italy would be an important source of immigrants as well.

But other settlers were having more troubles with the process of assimilation. Given its location across the river from the slave-holding state of Kentucky, Cincinnati saw its share of escaped and escaping slaves, along with owners or agents attempting to return them to their owners. Problems also arose when the city's free blacks were mistaken for escapees or were attacked for attempting to assist fugitives on their journey further north on the Underground Railroad. Whether free or fugitive, however, Cincinnati's African-American citizens invariably found themselves forced to live in the city's worst slum, labeled "Little Africa" or "Bucktown." Race riots were not uncommon, and culminated in the event of 1862, when Irish-led mobs, with some success, sought to drive blacks from the city. Yet Cincinnati was also home to some well-known figures who spoke out against slavery, most notably the Reverend Lyman Beecher, head of Lane Theological Seminary. His sister, Harriet Beecher Stowe, would publish one of the strongest pieces of anti-slavery literature in her novel *Uncle*

The University of Cincinnati's second
McMicken Hall (1940s) on the Clifton campus,
flanked by Hanna and Cunningham Halls.
(Courtesy of Cincinnati Historical Society)

Tom's Cabin (1852), inspired by conditions and incidents she observed while a resident in the Cincinnati area. In addition, students from Oberlin College and other institutions spent summers in Cincinnati, tutoring and otherwise assisting African-American residents in their struggles for equality, and some private schools intended for whites exhibited a willingness to accept as students a few "colored children of light hue."[1] In 1849 Cincinnati's African Americans won from the Ohio legislature the right to operate a system of public schools to educate black children, to be supported by taxes on black-owned businesses. This system was dissolved in 1874, in an attempt to effect a merger with the all-white Cincinnati Public Schools.[2] The merger existed only in principle, however, for in practice the public schools remained segregated for decades afterward.

Much could be written about the effect on Cincinnati of the Civil War, which began in 1861 with an attack on South Carolina's Fort Sumter by forces representing the Confederate States of America. In Cincinnati, serious conflicts arose between residents who favored the Northern position and those supporting the South, and the city's location left it open to attack by Confederate forces. In addition, the city's position at the boundary between slave and free states, its dependence on the Ohio River as the means by which its manufactured goods were shipped to out-of-state buyers, and its traditional ties to markets in the South were important factors in the beginning of Cincinnati's economic decline. However, General Lew Wallace put forces in position to protect the city, and Cincinnati factories, by turning out goods to fill the needs of the military, helped restore the city to a sounder economic base.

Yet despite a certain recovery, Cincinnati was unable to reclaim its pre-war title of "Queen City of the West." Indeed, the West was a much more extensive area than it had been before the war, with growing urban centers that would outdo Cincinnati in population, industry, and commerce. At the same time the South, facing losses in population and a decline in agricultural productivity, was in no position to reclaim its former status as Cincinnati's primary trade partner. Finally, shipping by water was being replaced by shipping by rail. Trains crossed the agricultural lands of the Midwest on routes established to the north of Cincinnati that would terminate in Chicago, St. Louis, and other, more westerly centers. In Cincinnati, now a somewhat smaller, less queenly Cincinnati, culture and the arts joined a revival of the city's prewar industrial base to return the city to its regal bearing.

EDUCATION, INDUSTRY AND THE ARTS

Even before mid-century, Cincinnati led the nation in some important developments that might be grouped under the heading of education. The city's Astronomical Society, founded by Ormsby Mitchell, financed their leader's trip to Europe to purchase a telescope. When he returned, Mitchell obtained land from Nicholas Longworth and, in 1843, brought John Quincy Adams to the city to speak at the ceremony that marked the laying of the cornerstone of Cincinnati's new observatory.[3] Cincinnati's citizens also organized such institutions as the Young Men's Mercantile Library in 1822, the Cincinnati Historical Society in 1844, the Cincinnati Law Library in 1846, and the Cincinnati Public Library in 1856.

Nor was the city lacking in institutions that provided formal education beyond the elementary grades. As early as 1806 Cincinnatians began to dream of establishing a city university. The process was slow and became a story of component parts that would eventually merge into a whole. The Medical College of Cincinnati, founded in 1819, would later become part of the university, as would the Ohio Mechanics Institute (founded in 1828), the Cincinnati Law School (1833), the Cincinnati College of Pharmacy (1850), the Cincinnati Conservatory of Music (1867), the College of Music (1878), and the McMicken School of Art and Design (1869). (The McMicken School would join the Cincinnati Art Museum on property in Eden Park in 1887.) The university proper held its first classes in Woodward High School in 1870, and moved to its own building, on a hillside near the intersection of Clifton and Vine, in 1875. It would begin occupying its current location in Clifton in 1895. In the next century the university added a pair of two-year colleges to its roster: Raymond Walters College, in suburban Blue Ash (1967), and Clermont College, in the county of the same name (1972). The University of Cincinnati joined the university system of the state of Ohio in 1977, and is currently an institution of some 38,000 students.

Sectarian institutions also marked Cincinnati's educational scene. Mount St. Mary's, a Catholic seminary, opened its doors in 1828, and Lane Theological Seminary, a Presbyterian institution, began operations in 1830. The Athenaeum, a Catholic college for men opened in 1831, was placed under the administration of the Jesuit Order in 1840, and grew into its modern form as Xavier University. Xavier also acquired what might be considered a sister institution, Our Lady of Cincinnati (1835, later rechristened Edgecliff College). In 1969 the merger of the two schools made Xavier University fully coeducational. Public and private schools throughout the city provided essential education for its children, and later in the century students were able to attend the city's first public high schools: Woodward, Hughes, and Walnut Hills.

It was becoming clear that Cincinnati was running out of space in the basin for its growing population and institutions. In what Daniel Hurley labels "the scramble up the hills,"[4] wealthy families began to build expansive homes in hilltop areas now known as Mt. Auburn, Avondale, Clifton, and Walnut Hills. Improvements in public transportation soon made possible a similar migration for middle-class citizens. Streetcars became more common, and the first of the city's inclined-plane railways opened in May of 1872. The Inclines, as they became known, would transport riders to Mt. Auburn (1872), Price Hill (1875), Bellevue (1876),

Mt. Adams (1876), and Fairview (1894). By 1948 all five had been torn down and replaced by more modern means of transportation.

At the same time the city began to provide new or expanded public services in the form of improved police protection, municipal water works and sewer lines, gaslights for its paved city streets, a post office, courts, and a professional fire department that became one of the country's most progressive. Between 1869 and 1918 Cincinnati extended these services and more to the new suburban areas as it annexed some 65 square miles of land and spread its boundaries into the surrounding hills. As well, the new Roebling Suspension Bridge, completed in 1867, provided easier access to areas of northern Kentucky and beyond.

Among the industries for which Cincinnati became home, Procter and Gamble, which moved to its Ivorydale headquarters in 1885, has surely been the best known and most diversified. It was in good company. By the 1880s the city was home to some 3,000 manufacturing establishments of various sizes and purposes. The regular trade fairs that drew visitors to the city during the years 1838-60 resumed after the Civil War with a series of larger and even more spectacular Industrial Expositions.

Developments in the arts also contributed to the economic recovery of post-Civil War Cincinnati. The city had become home to several builders of musical instruments, the best known of which was the Baldwin Piano Company, and retail stores selling

Pictures from left to right: Santiago (1908), a summer parlor streetcar. Similar cars were used in Cincinnati as early as 1898. The original University of Cincinnati, erected in 1875 on a hillside south of the broad bend of Clifton Avenue. The building was razed in 1935. McMicken Hall, first of the Clifton campus's buildings (1895). The Mount Adams Incline. (Courtesy of the Cincinnati and Hamilton County Public Library) A poster for the Fourth Cincinnati Industrial Exposition (1873). (Courtesy of Cincinnati Historical Society)

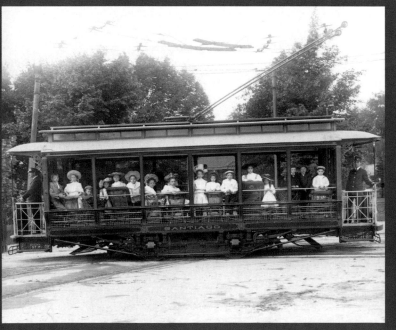

1873. CINCINNATI 1873.
INDUSTRIAL EXPOSITION

UNDER THE DIRECTION OF A BOARD OF COMMISSIONERS APPOINTED BY THE

Chamber of Commerce, Board of Trade, and Ohio Mechanics' Institute.

☞ THIS EXPOSITION IS SUPPORTED BY A PUBLIC GUARANTEE FUND, AND IS IN NO SENSE A PRIVATE ENTERPRISE. ☜

THE FOURTH EXPOSITION

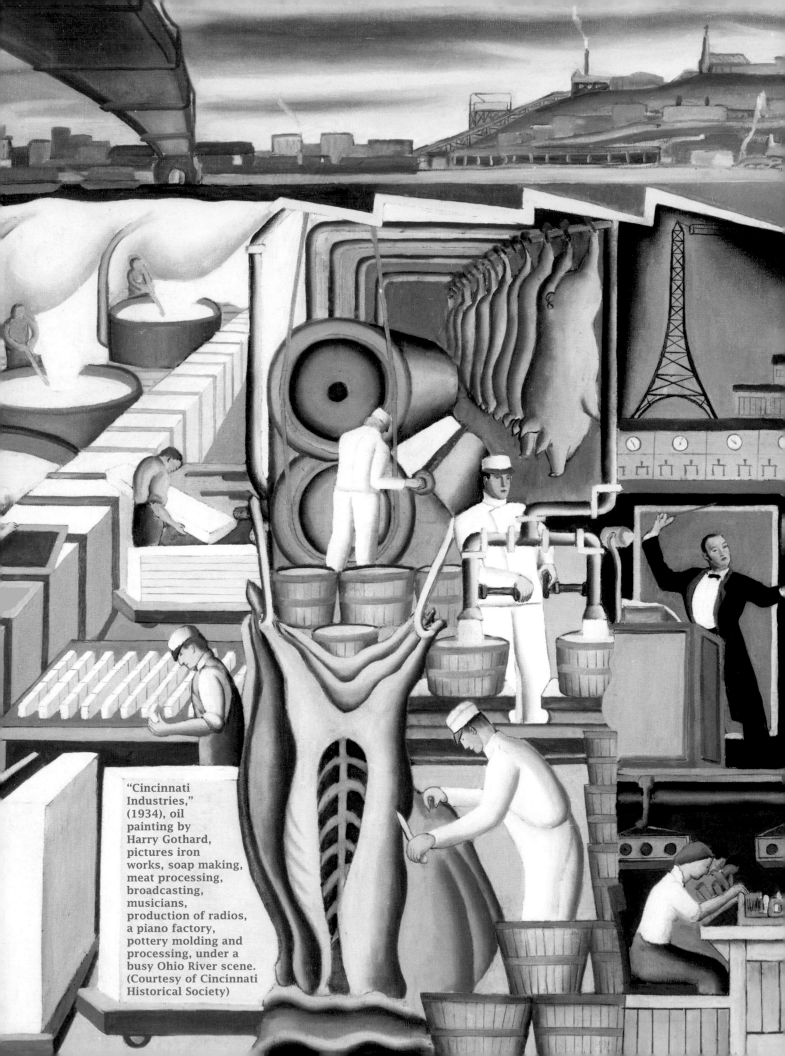

"Cincinnati Industries," (1934), oil painting by Harry Gothard, pictures iron works, soap making, meat processing, broadcasting, musicians, production of radios, a piano factory, pottery molding and processing, under a busy Ohio River scene. (Courtesy of Cincinnati Historical Society)

The main building of Procter and Gamble in "Ivorydale," a complex of offices and manufactories (ca. 1920), as seen from Spring Grove Avenue. (Courtesy of Cincinnati Historical Society)

instruments, sheet music, and related supplies prospered. America's largest theatrical publishing house and the respected music publisher John Church and Company had their headquarters here. Music teachers could be found throughout the city, and Cincinnati became recognized as a center of excellence for training in music and the visual arts. The Cincinnati Conservatory and the College of Music were gaining national reputations, and the Art Academy trained painters of wide renown. Women developed their artistic creativity in wood carving and art pottery. In 1880 Maria Longworth Nichols Storer founded the respected firm of Rookwood Pottery, one of the first major American businesses to be owned and operated by women. In the final decades of the nineteenth century Cincinnati cemented its position as one of America's cultural leaders with the founding of the still flourishing May Festival (1873), the Cincinnati Art Museum (1886) and its neighbor in Eden Park, the Cincinnati Art Academy (1887), and the Cincinnati Symphony Orchestra (1895). Music Hall, which opened its doors in 1878 with that year's May Festival, has since served as the home of Cincinnati's Symphony, its ballet company, and—since 1972—the Cincinnati Opera. Another important part of the city's culture, the sports scene, took to the spotlight in 1869, when the Cincinnati Red Stockings became America's first all-professional baseball team. Daniel Hurley summarizes the era succinctly.

"The cultural development accomplished [in post-Civil War Cincinnati] was as awesome in its way as the [city's] phenomenal growth had been a generation earlier. Parks and playgrounds, a music hall and an 'art palace,' festivals and expositions, and even a baseball team built civic pride...."[5]

One constant on the industrial scene was the city's many breweries. Cincinnati's first brewery opened in 1812, and the waves of German immigrants that dominated the numbers of new settlers in the later part of the century made the brewing of beer one of the city's identifying characteristics. By 1890 Cincinnati was known as the beer capital of the world; in 1892 city breweries produced some 1.3 million barrels of the golden liquid. But the institution of Prohibition in 1920 meant the end to prosperous times for the brewers. By the time Prohibition ended in 1933 there were few breweries left to reopen. A newcomer, Schoenling Brewing Co., opened in 1934, but by the 1970s it and Hudepohl were the only local breweries left. They were sold to an outside conglomerate in 1999. Recently, however, the name of nineteenth-century mega-brewer Christian Moerlein has appeared on a line of Cincinnati-made beers, and an old-fashioned beer garden is planned as part of the new construction on the Riverfront.

The decline of the brewing industry

Albert Valentien Supervising Rookwood Artists (ca. 1892). Rookwood's Mount Adams workshop eventually closed, but a new firm recently opened in Over-the-Rhine to carry on Rookwood's traditions. (Courtesy of Cincinnati Historical Society)

The Red Stockings

CHARLIE GOULD.
FIRST BASE.

GEO. WRIGHT.
SHORT STOP.

BRAINARD.

ANDY LEONARD.

FRED. WATERMAN.
3? BASE.

McVEY.
RIGHT FIELD.

23

was one symptom that the German character of Cincinnati was itself passing. In the course of the nineteenth century the number of Cincinnatians who could trace their origins to Germany had grown, reaching a peak by about 1890. In 1917, America's entry into World War I aroused some strong anti-German feelings from the rest of the city's population and with it demands that schools cease teaching the German language and that street names referring to German locales or persons be changed to something neutral: "German Street became English Street, Bremen became Republic, and Berlin became Woodrow."[6] German citizens, too, changed their surnames to sound more "American." The era of Prohibition meant not only the closing of German-owned breweries, but the saloons and beer gardens that had served as social centers for many German Americans.

The decade of the Great Depression was less traumatic for Cincinnati than for many other American cities due to the large number of moderate sized businesses and industries that contributed a certain stability to the labor force. However, the loss of jobs in the breweries could not be made up, even in the new and continuing projects that provided employment. The thirties saw the construction of some of the city's most distinctive and individual architecture: the

CAREW

TOWER

The Carew Tower, built in 1930, was Cincinnati's tallest building until 2011, when the Great American Tower was completed. (All pictures courtesy of Cincinnati Historical Society)

Carew Tower, the Netherland Plaza Hotel, the Downtown headquarters of Cincinnati Bell, the Times-Star Building, and Union Terminal (now the Museum Center). Even the Great Flood of 1937 did not destroy the city's spirit, and federal dollars supported new construction projects, slum clearance, and other public works, such as the public housing development Laurel Homes of 1937. Before the onset of World War II much anti-German sentiment had faded, but so had much of the German character that had marked the city for so long.

The city's government had also undergone some serious changes. Out of the disorganization of the post-Civil War era came a leader who would pull things together, for better or worse: George B. "Boss" Cox. Cox and his associates came to control the dispensation of government jobs and other political favors in the city and in Hamilton County, in exchange for payment from the recipients of these favors to support his organization. Cox's political machine instigated a well-lubricated system of patronage that prevailed in Cincinnati from the 1880s until Cox's death in 1916. Reform was slow to come, but finally took hold when a group of influential citizens, known as the Charter Committee, created a new city charter that voters approved in 1924. The system of government outlined in this document would

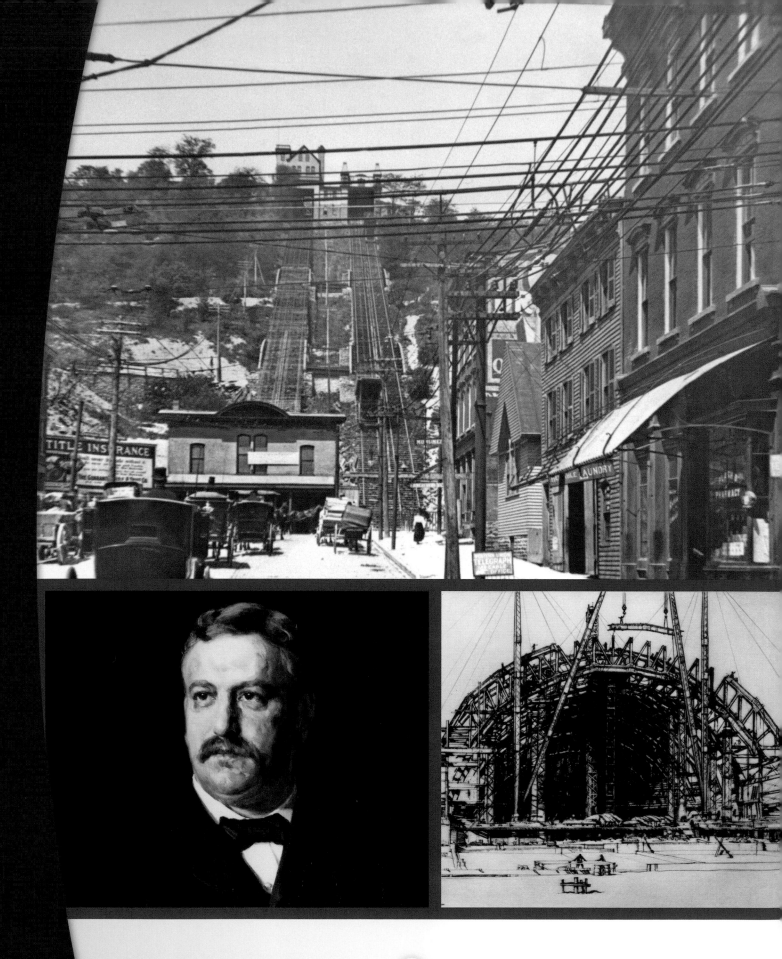

earn Cincinnati recognition as one of America's best-governed municipalities and a place on the National Municipal League's list of All-American Cities.

The economic recovery during and after World War II left the city's manufacturers and suppliers thriving, and developing modern methods of production to supply a burgeoning national market. Among the largest firms, Procter and Gamble became the world's foremost supplier of cleaning, personal health, and dental products, while General Electric turned a wartime piston engine factory into a producer of innovative jet engines for military and commercial customers. Ford and General Motors established manufacturing and assembly plants in and near Cincinnati, and the city's banks, insurance companies, and investment houses formed a support network for these and other growing industries. Their Downtown offices have been joined by new home headquarters of the Kroger Company, Federated Department Stores, Chiquita Brands, American Financial Corporation, Western and Southern Financial, 5/3 Bankcorp, Cincinnati Financial Corporation, and the latest incarnation of Procter and Gamble. Other distinguished businesses have their headquarters outside the downtown area but retain close connections to its people. These include Cincinnati Milacron, Rotex Global, and the Union Central Life Insurance Company.

Such commitment to the central city has given impetus to the growth of Downtown housing and the redevelopment of Cincinnati's original real estate, the Riverfront. Impressive

Pictures from left to right: The Price Hill Incline (opened 1874; photo ca. 1914) was the only one to use double tracks: one for passengers, the other for freight; portrait of George B. "Boss" Cox by Henry Mosler; Union Terminal under construction and completed (1933); downtown headquarters of Cincinnati Bell, designed by Harry Hake (1931). (All pictures courtesy of Cincinnati Historical Society)

28

Downtown Cincinnati during the Great Flood of January, 1937. The Ohio River crested at 80 feet, leaving over 60,000 Cincinnatians homeless. (Picture by M. Parks Watson, courtesy of Cincinnati Historical Society)

new condominium and rental towers overlook parkland that stretches east from the Downtown area, and fans flock to Paul Brown Stadium and the Great American Ballpark, facilities for Cincinnati's professional football and baseball teams. Future construction between these venues, an area known as The Banks, will include commercial and residential developments, a new park, and an entertainment district. Work has already begun on a casino, situated to the northeast of Downtown. Further north, the reconfiguration of Washington Park, one of the city's oldest green spaces, will complement the School for Creative and Performing Arts and a renovated Music Hall.

Symbolic of developments in Cincinnati's urban core is the recently opened Great American Tower, erected Downtown on a property dubbed Queen City Square. This skyscraper, commissioned by the Western and Southern Financial Group, tops the Cincinnati skyline at 41 stories and 660 feet, 86 feet higher than the city's former tallest structure, the Carew Tower. It is also the city's first "green" building. This regal addition to Downtown's skyline is topped by a brightly lit ornament modeled on a tiara once worn by Britain's Princess Diana, an appropriate symbol of the newest face of the Queen City of the West.

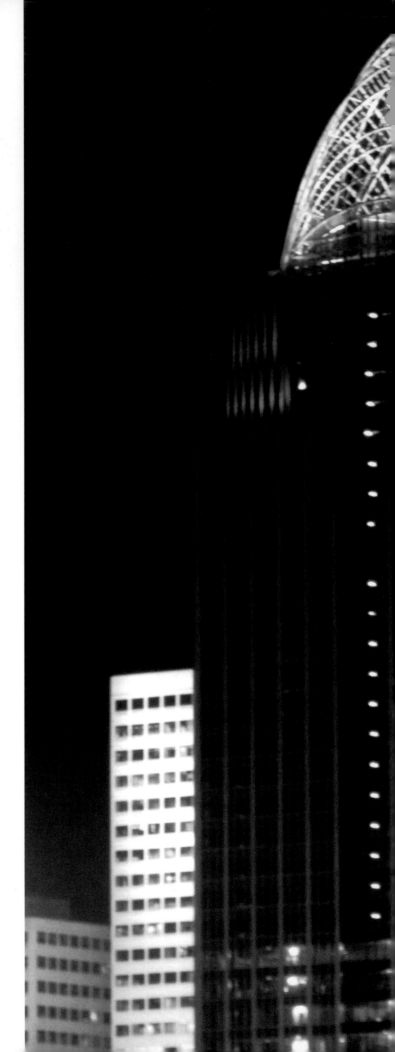

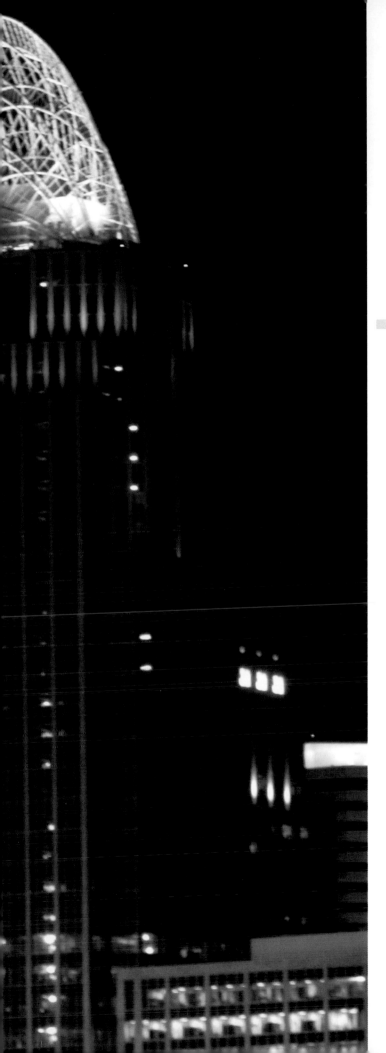

Cincinnati's newest and tallest skyscraper, the Great American Tower, topped by the brightly lit royal tiara. (Courtesy of Wikipedia)

NOTES

1. Charles Theodore Greve, *Centennial History of Cincinnati and Representative Citizens* (Chicago: Biographical Publishing Company, 1904), I:887.

2. Authorized by the state legislature in 1825, the Cincinnati Public Schools (then known as the Common Schools of Cincinnati) had grown into a sizeable system by the end of the century. The city's first Catholic school opened in 1825, the result of efforts by French nuns called to Cincinnati to begin this work. By 1900, Catholic schools were flourishing.

3. The area in which the Observatory was built was renamed Mount Adams in honor of the guest speaker. In 1873 the Observatory was moved further east, to an area now called Mount Lookout.

4. The title of Chapter 3 of Hurley's *Cincinnati, the Queen City* (Cincinnati: Cincinnati Historical Society, 1982).

5. Ibid., 62.

6. Ibid., 105.

Queen City of Song:
CHORAL MUSIC IN CINCINNATI'S SCHOOLS, CONSERVATORIES, AND *Universities*

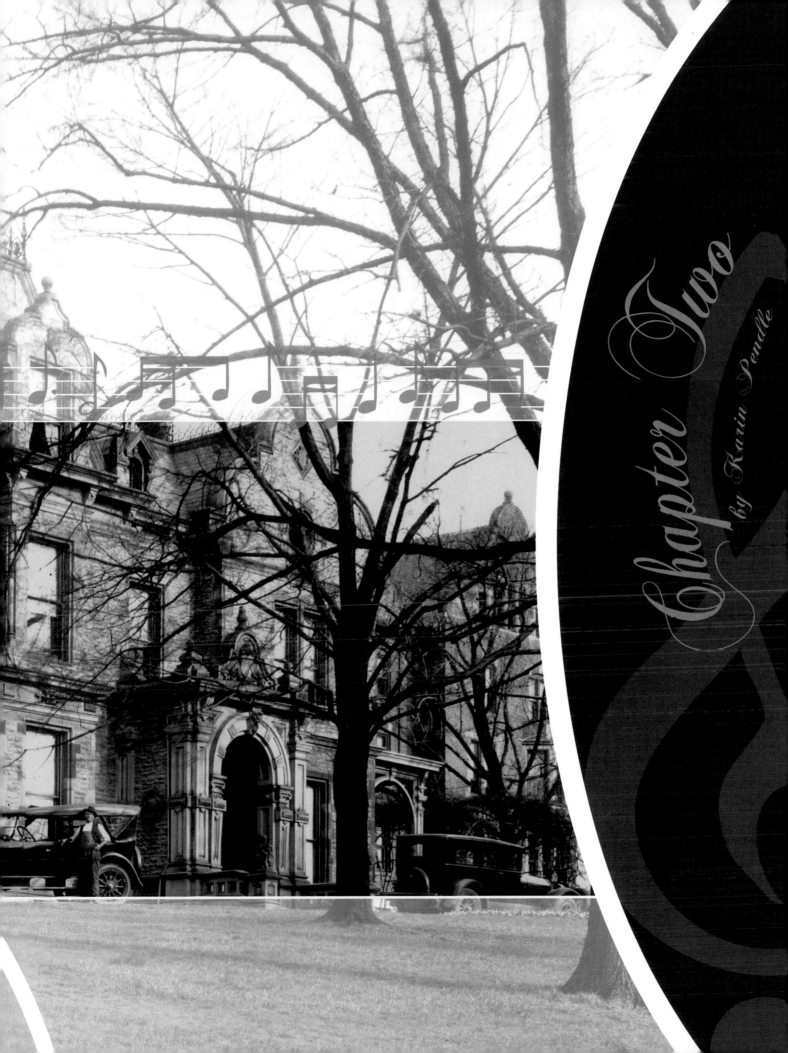

Why Cincinnati? Why and how did this city come to be associated with the cultivation of choral music? To be sure, Cincinnati has long been considered a center for the making and enjoyment of music. Since the late nineteenth century it has supported major schools of music, a symphony orchestra of international reputation, a summer opera season, concert series to appeal to many tastes, even recording facilities used by major figures in popular music and jazz. And the venerable May Festival, established in 1873 and still the United States's longest continuing choral festival, surely heads the list of important choral presences in the nation. Yet the city's background is as distinguished as its foreground. Singing societies, community choruses, and church music establishments—both white and African American—dotted the city landscape even before the founding of its two distinguished music schools—the Cincinnati Conservatory in 1867, the College of Music in 1878—added greater professionalism to the musical scene, even as the May Festival was defining its character and the Cincinnati Symphony Orchestra (1895) played its first season. Thus many developments support the reputation of Cincinnati as a center for the cultivation of choral music. However, one important source fed all the rest: the early and continuing programs of music education in the city's public and parochial schools.

An early entrant among projects undertaken to settle the newly acquired Northwest Territory of the United States, the village of Cincinnati was founded in 1788 on the banks of the Ohio River, opposite the mouth of Kentucky's Licking River. Its location at first prompted the founders to name it Losantiville (literally, city opposite the mouth of the L[icking River]). Not long afterward, people began thinking about education for the city's growing number of children. Many of the new schools were small and did not survive for long; many were single-sex private academies where tuition was charged and student enrollment was small; others were free and open to the public, though not part of any government-supported system; most were intended for white students only and did not go beyond the elementary grades. Records are silent, however, on whether any of these schools excelled in music or even cultivated music in their curricula.

Meanwhile, forces in Columbus, the seat of Ohio's state government, were being put in play that would bring important changes to the position of public education. In 1825 the legislature authorized a half-mill tax to support a system of public schools. By 1829 Cincinnati had the makings of such a system in place: the Common Schools of Cincinnati. Governed at first by a Board of Trustees (renamed the Board of Education in 1868), the Board hired its first superintendent, Nathan Guilford, in 1850. Guilford and his immediate successor, Joseph Merrill, were elected by popular vote, but by 1853 the Board became authorized to appoint its own superintendent. Starting with four rather ill-equipped schools, the system grew in size and quality as public interest and trust in the importance of education increased and enrollment grew.[1]

However, two basic weaknesses needed to be addressed: the first schools covered only grades 1-8, and the system was intended for white students and teachers only.

Until 1849 there were no publicly funded secondary schools in Ohio; but in Cincinnati two important benefactors, William Woodward and Thomas Hughes, would soon provide the city with its first high schools. Money and property from the estates of these men paid, wholly or in part, for these schools, which would eventually fall under the jurisdiction of Cincinnati's Board of Education: Woodward High School (opened in 1831) and Hughes High School (opened in 1853). Woodward moved in 1855 to the property eventually occupied, from 1976 to 2010, by the School for Creative and Performing Arts, also a public institution, and relocated to Reading Road in Bond Hill in 1953.[2] Hughes moved from the West End to a new building, erected on Clifton Avenue in 1908-11, which—with renovations and extensions—is still in use. Until the end of the nineteenth century these two schools, along with Walnut Hills High School (1895, then located at Burdett and Ashland Avenues), served most of the city's students of high school age.[3]

Though public schools for African Americans had existed in Cincinnati as early as 1820, the black students who could afford them were being educated in private academies, supported by tuition, fees, and contributions from parents and supporters.

However, in 1849 the state legislature gave Cincinnati's African Americans the right to organize an Independent Colored School System, which was supported by taxes on black-owned property and administered by an all-black school board. In 1866 the Colored Schools added Gaines High School to their number. In 1874 Cincinnati's all-white Board of Education took over the administration of the Colored Schools, supposedly to facilitate racial integration of the educational system as a whole. Nevertheless, and even after 1887, when the Ohio legislature outlawed segregation in public education, most African-American students in Cincinnati still attended predominantly or completely black schools. By 1901 over half the school-age African Americans had pulled out of the public schools in favor of private institutions.[4] During these years some determined teachers pushed for and finally established music as part of the curricula of Cincinnati Public Schools.

MUSIC COMES TO PUBLIC EDUCATION

he fact [is]...that our pupils can sing, and that they learned the art of singing in the public schools."[5]

And sing they did. Choruses of school children frequently performed for businessmen or industrialists who came to Cincinnati for regional or national meetings. Children's voices helped celebrate important civic occasions and sang at commemorations of historical events. In 1859 and 1860, as many as 600 students from the city's intermediate and high schools participated in fund-raising music festivals to benefit the public library. In 1878 and 1879 the

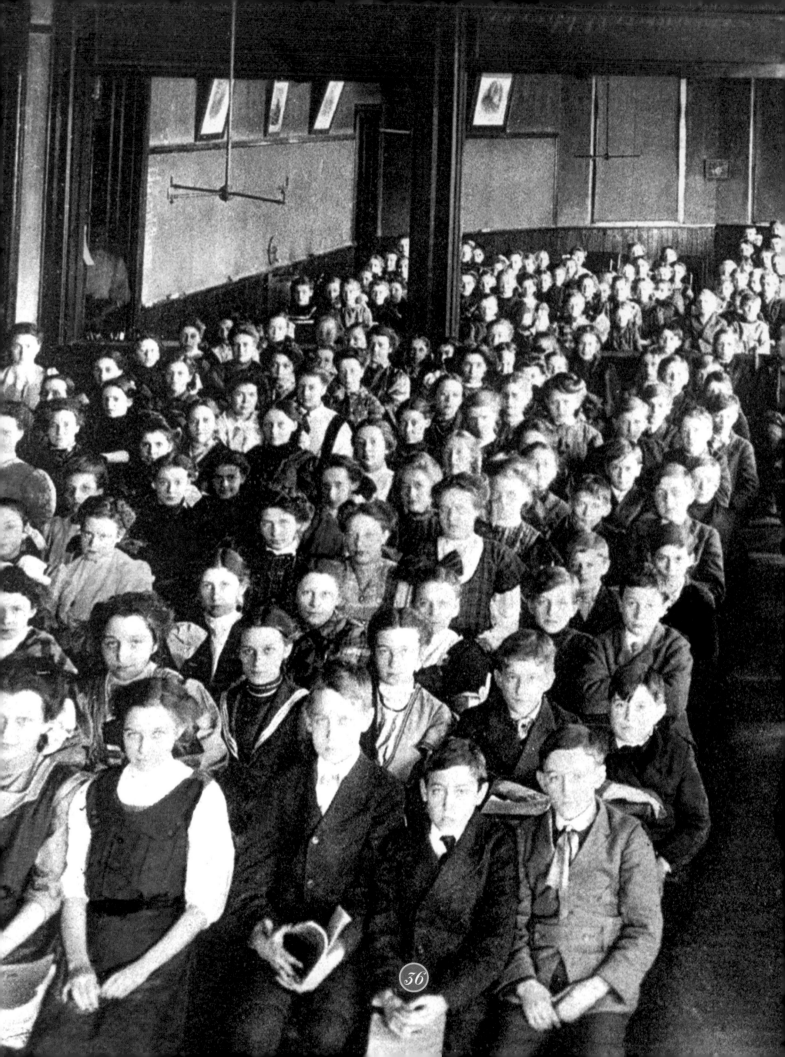

A chorus of Cincinnati school children wait to
go onstage for a 1908 May Festival concert.
They sang in Bach's *St. Matthew Passion* and
Pierné's *The Children's Crusade.* (Courtesy of
Cincinnati Memory Project)

voices of school children were raised for the cause of scholarships for middle and secondary students to take lessons at the College of Music of Cincinnati. In 1908 the children gathered to present a concert of German folk songs, and in 1909 some 800 children, accompanied by orchestra, presented *Our Lincoln,* a festal ode by Cincinnati Public School music teacher Joseph Surdo and principal W. C. Washburn.[6] After 1900, when many of the city's schools had their own auditoriums, students were heard in cantatas and other large-scale works, and as participants in operettas and musical revues.[7] The new medium of radio provided opportunities for school groups to be broadcast locally, even nationally, over Cincinnati's WLW, one of the nation's first clear channel stations.

Programs of the Cincinnati Symphony

Orchestra often included contributions by combined choirs from the city's schools. In 1905, for example, a city-wide boys' choir performed with the orchestra, and in the 1930s students from the city's high schools regularly participated in the orchestra's annual Christmas concerts.[8] However, perhaps the appearances of massed school choirs most valued by Cincinnatians were those in the then-biennial May Festivals.[9] At the first May Festivals (1873 and 1875) a large chorus of pupils and teachers from the city's intermediate, secondary, and normal schools presented music learned in their public school classes. Beginning in 1882, planners of the festivals began working student choral ensembles into the regular festival repertoire, such as Bach's *St. Matthew Passion,* Berlioz's *Damnation of Faust* and *Te Deum,* Handel's *Judas Maccabeus,* or

Pictures from left to right: The second location of Woodward High School, 1854-55. The earliest location of Walnut Hills High School, 1895. Title page, *First Annual Report...for the Colored Public Schools* (1855). Hughes High School's first location, on W. Fifth Street. (Courtesy of Cincinnati Historical Society and Cincinnati Memory Project)

FIRST ANNUAL REPORT

OF THE

BOARD OF TRUSTEES,

FOR THE

COLORED PUBLIC SCHOOLS

OF CINCINNATI,

For the School Year, ending June 30, 1855;

WITH ADDITIONAL DOCUMENTS, EXHIBITING THE CONDITION OF
THE COLORED SCHOOLS.

Printed by Order of the Board.

CINCINNATI:
MOORE, WILSTACH, KEYS & CO.,
NO. 25 WEST FOURTH STREET.
1855.

Rubinstein's *Tower of Babel.* In 1897 a Children's May Festival, utilizing some 2,000 students from the city schools, presented Franz Abt's *Cinderella.* Peter Benoit's cantata *Into the World*, with a chorus of 700 school children accompanied by the Cincinnati Symphony Orchestra under Frank Van der Stucken, first appeared on programs of 1906, and was repeated in 1912 and 1927. Between 1908 and 1952, Gabriel Pierné's oratorios *The Children's Crusade, The Children at Bethlehem,* and *St. Francis of Assisi*, all involving children, enjoyed repeated performances.[10] Choruses of school children continue to be welcome participants in such major works as Orff's *Carmina Burana,* Walton's *Belshazzar's Feast,* Mahler's Symphony No. 3, and Britten's *War Requiem.* All these accomplishments would have been impossible had not Cincinnati schools, both public and parochial, introduced music into their curricula.

Indeed, the cultivation of choral music in the Cincinnati Public Schools had a long and distinguished history. Soon after the establishment of the Cincinnati Common Schools, the city's cultural organizations and interested individuals proposed that music become a regular feature of their curricula. In 1834, for example, the Eclectic Academy of Music began working to promote music

as a suitable subject to be taught in the schools. Likewise, speakers at meetings of the Western Literary Institute and the College of Professional Teachers addressed such topics as "Vocal Music as a Branch of Common School Education." In fact, vocal music was the only kind advocated by these champions and the only kind eventually added to grade-school curricula.[11]

The years 1837-38 appear to have seen the first actual music classes in the schools, probably taught by T. B. Mason, though music had not yet become a regular part of grade school instruction. In 1842 Charles Aiken established free music classes for children in the basement of Sixth Presbyterian Church, and several music teachers worked in the schools without pay until 1844, when W. F. Colburn and Mrs. E. K. Thatcher became the system's first paid instructors of music. Charles Aiken himself joined the faculty of Hughes and Woodward High Schools and would, in 1871, become Cincinnati Public Schools' first Superintendent of Music.

To be sure, there were those who opposed taking time in the school day to study music, something they deemed frivolous. They might well have looked askance when Aiken or his successor, Gustav

Junkermann, said simply that the central purpose of school music classes was to teach children to sing well and to cultivate their ability to sight-read music, whether in unison or in part-songs. Yet justifying the inclusion of music in school curricula seldom dealt with such immediately practical ends. Rather, music study was justified as fulfilling higher purposes: the cultivation of moral behavior and right thinking, disciplining the mind, and educating the emotions.[12]

Vocal music retained its leading place in public school music throughout the nineteenth century and did not lose its primacy even when school bands and orchestras were gaining favor in the first half of the twentieth century. For this reason alone, performing choral music would attract many students who wished to continue some musical activity after their formal education ended, and the Cincinnati Public Schools made this possible by instructing

Far left: bust of Charles Aiken, Cincinnati Public Schools' first Superintendent of Music, by Preston Powers, now in Music Hall lobby. (Photo by Frank Pendle) Above left to right: Charles Aiken; Walter Aiken, Superintendent of Music 1900-30; Louis Aiken, music teacher at Hughes High School. (Courtesy of Cynthia Perin Annett)

A division of the Cincinnati Boychoir, 2003-04. (Courtesy of Cincinnati Boychoir)

Clark and Gamble School students are taught according to principles developed by Italian educator Maria Montessori, while the School for Creative and Performing Arts offers pre-professional instruction in music, drama, dance, creative writing, visual arts, and theatre technology alongside such traditional academic subjects as English, social studies, science, math, and modern languages, and accepts students from elementary grades through high school. The newly rebuilt Taft High School focuses on information technology, while Withrow International High School offers programs in world languages and international business and certification in the International Baccalaureate program. Woodward High School provides career-oriented instruction in the technologies of manufacturing, construction, and health care. Walnut Hills High School offers the city's most rigorous college preparatory curriculum, while Schroder, also a college prep high school, uses the Paideia method of instruction, based on techniques of critical thinking. Other Cincinnati schools emphasize specific languages—e.g., the Clifton-Fairview German School.[21] Space does not permit full discussion of each school. Instead, three schools offering noteworthy choral experiences will serve as examples of the best that Cincinnati has to

Some members of the Senior Ensemble.
(Courtesy of Dan Ledbetter)

offer: Walnut Hills High School, the School for Creative and Performing Arts, and the suburban Winton Woods High School.

Walnut Hills was Cincinnati's third public high school, joining Woodward and Hughes High Schools in 1895, and is the city's only high school to be ranked repeatedly among the best in the United States.[22] Each year it educates some 1900 students in grades 7-12 in what the school handbook describes as "a classical six-year college preparatory" curriculum offering "rigorous college preparatory courses, as well as college level courses, enabling students to graduate with advanced standing" and "continu[ing] to serve as a model of excellence in the educational community" in its traditional role as a unique college preparatory secondary school. Walnut Hills offers more Advance Placement courses than any other school in the country as well as the largest program of extracurricular activities in Cincinnati. The student body, drawn from across the city, is fully integrated: 58.9% white, 38.3% minorities (African-American, Hispanic, and Asian); and largely middle class.[24]

Walnut Hills High School's "magnet" character is of long standing. By 1915 sixty percent of its graduates went on to college, leading Cincinnati's superintendent of schools, Randall Condon, to suggest that the institution develop an identity as the city's classical college preparatory institution. In 1935, 1972, and 1996 the Cincinnati Board of Education "reaffirmed the status of the school as a six-year program specialized for college prep."[25] Its graduation requirements are clearly specified and strongly academic, designed to meet the entrance requirements of nearly any American college or university. Among them are a semester course in vocal or instrumental music in grade 7 or 8 and a Fine Arts credit, chosen from music, art, or speech and theatre offerings, sometime during grades 9-12.[26] Walnut Hills' five-member music department offers a wealth of music performance options, along with an AP course in Music Theory that is comparable in content to freshman theory courses at many colleges.

Lisa Peters, choral director at Walnut Hills since 2001, leads a well developed program that allows students to progress in ability and experience from the time they enter the school. The Beginning Choir serves about 100 seventh, eighth, and ninth graders each semester and deals with the basics of good choral singing: "posture, tone, intonation, blend and balance," along with music fundamentals (music-reading skills and terminology).[27] In all her classes Peters also teaches good rehearsal techniques, encouraging students to think as a group and work toward common musical goals. Members of the Beginning Choir may go on to the more advanced Junior Choir, which serves those in grades 8 and 9. Their repertoire, largely four-part *a cappella* music, covers a wide range of styles. For both these choirs Peters chooses techniques and repertoire suited to training

the male changing voice. The Beginning and Junior Choirs present public concerts.

Tenth graders may be admitted to the Boys or Girls Chorus, each of 35-50 students, or may be chosen, along with students in grades 11 and 12, for the 40-voice Senior Choir. Repertoire for this choir is on a par with that of many college choirs, and most members study voice privately. By graduation, all student singers will have the training and experience to participate in community and church choirs or other vocal ensembles for the rest of their lives.

In addition to performing in school concerts, Walnut Hills' vocal ensembles regularly appear with the Cincinnati Symphony and Cincinnati Pops orchestras in subscription concerts and in the annual May Festival. They also perform at churches and other locations in the city. They have sung with the Vocal Arts Ensemble, a professional choir, and with the chorus of the Cincinnati Opera, and have toured to cities in the United States and abroad. In their choirs, as in their academic work, Walnut Hills's students are continually challenged to live up to their school's motto, *Sursum ad summum*, "Rise to the highest."

Winton Woods High School serves the northern Cincinnati suburbs of Greenhills, Forest Park, and Springfield Township. In addition to a traditional academic curriculum that includes opportunities for Honors, AP, and online studies, the school provides courses in vocal and instrumental music, technology, art, graphic design, and more. Winton Woods also offers a large roster of extracurricular activities and a full program of

Top: The Varsity Ensemble of
Winton Woods High School.
Bottom: Winton Woods High
School, main entrance.

Winton Woods singers and conductor David
Bell perform in China to celebrate the 2008
Olympics. The Great Wall is in the background.
(Courtesy of Theresa Cleary)

一世界同一个梦想

World One Dream

55

athletics.[28] A new division of the high school, the Academy of Global Studies, is only the third program in the country to offer a global perspective in all its courses. The Academy's fine arts component is under the leadership of the school's head choral conductor, David Bell. All Winton Woods schools are racially integrated, and the district, largely middle class, serves some 3500 students.

The choral program of Winton Woods High School features groups of various sizes that cover a broad spectrum of repertoire to appeal to students of differing tastes and talents. The Varsity Ensemble, a mixed-voice choir of about 50 members directed by David Bell, is the school's top choir. This group has appeared frequently with the Cincinnati Symphony and Cincinnati Pops Orchestras and is featured on two Pops recordings. Cincinnati audiences have also heard them as guests in the University of Cincinnati's Feast of Carols and on television broadcasts aired on local outlets. They also appeared on the national PBS broadcast "Fourth of July from the Heartland" with the Pops in 2000. They consistently receive the highest ratings in district and statewide competitions. In 2008 the Varsity Ensemble traveled to China, where they performed in the concert hall of the Forbidden City as part of a "Salute to the Beijing Olympics."

Cincinnati composer Dan Landau has written several pieces for special appearances by Winton Woods choirs, including "Farewell Song" for the closing of Cincinnati's Tall Stacks celebration of 1995, "Light the Fire Within" for the 2001 Olympic Torch Relay Ceremony, and a song for Opening Day of the Cincinnati Reds' season in 2007. Other pieces for Winton Woods have come from composers Cynthia Gray ("Where Earth Meets Sky"), David Brunner ("This We Know"), and Sherri Porterfield ("The White Moon," on a text by French poet Paul Verlaine).

The school year 2011-12 marks conductor David Bell's thirtieth year as head of Winton Woods High School's choral staff. His classroom work has been recognized in nationally circulated journals, and in 2008 he was named Teacher of the Year by Winton Woods City Schools. Bell was a member of the founding committee of Cincinnati's May Festival Youth Chorus and has served as president of the Ohio Choral Directors Association. He holds degrees from Northern Illinois University and the University of Cincinnati. Assistant Conductor Elizabeth Barth, a graduate of Virginia's College of William and Mary and Indiana University, is in charge of Winton Woods' Women's Chorale and Men's Choir. She also leads the extracurricular *a cappella* groups *Evolution* and *Countless Harmony*, both ensembles of 12-16 voices that specialize in contemporary and improvisational idioms.[29] Taken together, Winton Woods High School's choral program involves about 250 students each year.

The Winton Woods Music Boosters, a volunteer group of parents, supports all the district's school music groups by publicizing their performances and accomplishments and by raising funds, primarily by running concession stands at school athletic competitions. They also award a scholarship every year to an outstanding music student. The Boosters have assisted Winton Woods' choral groups and their able conductors in building what has been recognized as one of the best high school choral programs in Ohio.

The opening, in August of 2010, of the newest—and most likely the final—facility for Cincinnati's School for Creative and Performing Arts (SCPA) was in all ways an occasion for great celebration. This thoroughly modern public facility consolidated the former SCPA (grades 4-12), founded in 1973, and Schiel Primary School for Arts Enrichment (grades K-3), established in 1985. Together these schools became the first public arts-oriented educational institutions in the United States to serve students from kindergarten through twelfth grade. SCPA programs include not only training in all areas of vocal and instrumental music, but drama, theatre technology, creative writing, dance, and visual arts, coupled with a college preparatory academic curriculum of recognized quality. Students are accepted into these programs on the basis of successful auditions and/or interviews.

Like all Cincinnati high schools, the School for Creative and Performing Arts draws students, some 1350 strong, from the entire city; qualified students from outside city limits (about 3% of those admitted) may attend on payment of tuition. The student body is Greater Cincinnati's most diverse,

encompassing those of white, African-American, Hispanic, Asian, Native American, and multi-racial heritages, from wealthy, middle-class, and low income families. The campaign to raise money for the new school, spearheaded by the late Cincinnati Pops conductor Erich Kunzel, brought in over $31 million in private donations to match the public funds available. Once again the people of Cincinnati showed their strong support for the arts, at a time when school levies seemed to be failing more often than they passed. This level of support is reflected in the first item of the school's Vision Statement: "SCPA strives to become a school where standard funding is consistently and substantially augmented by the financial support of arts donors, corporations, and foundations."[30] In its new location the School for Creative and Performing Arts joins Music Hall, Memorial Hall, the Art Academy of Cincinnati, Ensemble Theatre, and Know Theatre as part of what looks increasingly like a central arts location in the core of the city.

The nature of the school, along with the wide range in ages among its students, has resulted in a varied program of opportunities for choruses and small vocal ensembles. Led by instructors Rick Hand and Laurie Wyant-Zenni, about 40 students from grades 4-7 form "Voices of SCPA." Here they learn the principles of good choral singing, along with rehearsal and performance techniques, in repertoire for two- and three-part treble voices. The Children's Choir, also about 40 students from grades 4-7, is a more advanced continuation of "Voices." Students in grades 7-9 sing in the Junior High Choir or the

Advanced Junior High Choir, where they master repertoire for mixed voices. Singers of high-school age may join the Women's Ensemble or the Chorale; the latter performs advanced high-school and collegiate level repertoire.

Membership in smaller, more specialized groups like the *Baby Grands, Meridian 8,* and *Tremolo* requires an audition. Wyant's *Baby Grands* is an *a cappella* ensemble for female voices that performs both classical and popular music. Hand's *Meridian 8* concentrates on vocal jazz, both accompanied and *a cappella*. *Tremolo*, for male singers of high school age, sings *a cappella* repertoire of varied genres, under the leadership of Ms. Wyant. SCPA's choral ensembles have been recognized both locally and nationally for their quality. *Baby Grands* and *Tremolo* have brought home awards from the Verona (Italy) International Choral Competition and the Festival Disney National Vocal Competition. The Advanced Junior High Choir consistently receives superior ratings in events sponsored by the Ohio Music Education Association. SCPA ensembles have appeared frequently with the Cincinnati Symphony Orchestra, the Cincinnati Pops, and the Vocal Arts Ensemble, and have been invited to sing in events sponsored by the choral department at the University of Cincinnati's College-Conservatory of Music. Clearly, Cincinnati's School for Creative and Performing Arts is providing its students with many opportunities to fulfill the school's motto: "Find Your Voice."

Picture captions for the previous pages: A young member of a choir of the School for Creative and Performing Arts. A children's choir from the SCPA. The May Festival Youth Choir performs in the Festival. Main entrance of the Erich Kunzel Center for the Performing Arts. (Courtesy of Frank Pendle)

CHORAL MUSIC IN THE ROMAN CATHOLIC SCHOOLS OF CINCINNATI

The Roman Catholic school system of Southwest Ohio was the result of the work of several forces within what is now the Archdiocese of Cincinnati.[31] The original diocese, established in 1821 under the leadership of Bishop Edward Fenwick, included the states of Ohio, Michigan, and other areas of America's Northwest Territories. As the population of the diocese increased, the area was subdivided into several smaller administrative units; by the mid-twentieth century the Cincinnati area, now an Archdiocese, would encompass a total of nineteen counties surrounding the city, an area of 8,543 square miles, and could boast of an educational system consisting of 200 elementary and high schools, five colleges and universities, and ten seminaries, established and maintained by a number of Catholic teaching orders. From the beginning, choral music was included in their curricula.

The first Roman Catholic school in the Archdiocese of Cincinnati was established in 1824 by an order of French nuns as an adjunct to the city's only Catholic church. By mid-century enrollment in the parochial schools had tripled, as more churches were established and opened their own schools. By the mid-twentieth century over 42,000 of the Archdiocese's children were enrolled in Catholic schools. Though financial considerations and the gradual migration of families from cities to suburbs led to the closing or consolidation of some of these schools, they remain a force to be reckoned with in society and in the field of music education.

Until about 1900 the aims of music instruction in Catholic schools were similar to those of the public schools. Teachers wanted to turn out capable singers who knew the fundamentals of music and who could sight-read as members of a choral group. In the course of the nineteenth century, however, the movement toward church music reform gained momentum, and Pope Pius X, in his *Moto proprio* of 1903, laid out the principles by which music in the church would be governed. In Cincinnati, students in the Catholic schools were increasingly taught these principles and put into service as church musicians. Gregorian chant was declared the model against which all other church music was to be judged, and even students in the lower grades of elementary school were taught to sing this liturgical music. Composers of polyphonic church music, such as Cincinnati's Martin Dumler, a graduate of the College of Music, created Masses and motets that were approved for use within schools and churches. Both the College of Music and the Cincinnati Conservatory offered courses on the boy choir, and the Conservatory developed a joint program in church music with the Athenaeum of Ohio, a Catholic seminary. Finally, in 1926—a century after the first Catholic school opened in the Archdiocese—John J. Fehring was appointed the first Diocesan Supervisor of Music and asked to formulate a standard course of study for the schools. The emphasis was to be on vocal/choral music.

By 1944 the Catholic high schools had choirs capable of singing liturgical or secular repertoire. In 1946, a typical year, massed school choirs participated in Marian Day programs, concerts of Christmas carols and other repertoire, and Holy Week services. Demonstration Masses, as many as three per year, involved choruses of a thousand or more students. Nine hundred fifth and sixth graders sang Mass at St. Monica's Church in Cincinnati, and a choral group from the Archdiocese sang for the National Catholic Music Teachers Convention in Cleveland. Catholic school students participated in the May Festival, and high school choirs caroled on Cincinnati's Fountain Square. Spring concerts in Catholic schools featured student choirs along with student instrumental groups.

Throughout its history, choral music in the Catholic schools of the city had a mutual relationship with choral music in the churches, contributing to reciprocal developments in both areas.

Many changes brought about by the Second Vatican Council (October 11, 1962-December 8, 1965) affected music in the Roman Catholic churches of the Cincinnati Archdiocese, which led in turn to changes in school music. In an attempt to encourage more involvement by church members in worship, the Council encouraged the use of vernacular languages rather than Latin, and Gregorian chant was replaced on the local level with whatever music the local churches deemed to be in keeping with the spirit of their services. Though use of the organ was encouraged, other instruments were to be admitted as well. Thus, training school children in the traditional ways of church music yielded place to music in more familiar idioms, with text in the language of the everyday.

CHORAL MUSIC AT CINCINNATI'S INSTITUTIONS OF HIGHER LEARNING

The Cincinnati Conservatory of Music

The University of Cincinnati's College-Conservatory of Music (CCM), the city's largest and most prestigious institution for advanced musical training, resulted from the merger of three component parts: the Cincinnati Conservatory of Music, the College of Music of Cincinnati, and the University of Cincinnati itself. Though the three did not complete this merger until 1962, all had acquired long and distinguished histories that began with their separate origins in the nineteenth century. In 1867 Clara Baur, a German immigrant and music teacher, founded her embryonic conservatory in rented quarters in Miss [Clara] Nourse's School for Young Ladies.[32] Miss Baur was not the first to open a music studio in the city, nor was Miss Nourse's the first school to include a music component. But Baur's aims went beyond the simple studio: she dreamed of a German-style conservatory modeled after her own school in Stuttgart and staffed by European-trained performer-teachers of the highest sort. Besides herself, the fledgling conservatory's faculty included Caroline Rivé (voice), Michael Brand

(strings), and Henry Andres (piano), all of them born and/or trained in Europe.

Having outgrown the space allotted to it in Miss Nourse's academy and the additional rooms Miss Baur had been able to rent, the Conservatory moved to the two upper stories of a three-story downtown building. Twice more it outgrew its quarters, and Miss Baur looked further, this time outside the downtown area, where her Conservatory could have a home that was truly permanent. This she found in the vacant mansion and surrounding property in Mount Auburn that had been the home of the Shillito family. After some remodeling, the new Conservatory was ready. In 1902 Miss Baur, her faculty of thirty, and the student body of around a thousand moved up the hill to the property at Highland and Oak Streets, which would be their home, and the home of the eventually consolidated College-Conservatory of Music, until their merger with the University of Cincinnati and the eventual move to its Clifton campus in 1967.

Choral music had been part of the Conservatory's offerings ever since it had enrolled sufficient students to make a chorus possible. However, the student body remained predominantly female for some time, which somewhat limited the possible repertoire. Even as late as the 1896-97 school year, when the Conservatory enrolled 876 students, only 53 were male. Enrollment in the six-week summer school, established in 1868 to provide public school music teachers with a way to update their skills, was also predominantly female. However, it became traditional for these students to form a summer chorus and, most years, to give a concert as part of Commencement exercises. In 1877 a Conservatory-sponsored mixed chorus that included members of the community rehearsed in the evening. George Magrath, who joined the faculty in 1878, further developed the Conservatory Chorus, and a women's chorus, conducted by Clara Baur, then by Frederic Shailer Evans, became a regular offering in 1885. A men's chorus, which probably involved both students and townspeople, followed in 1892. In the 1890s a women's vocal ensemble, the Conservatory Double Quartet—also under Evans—is known to have performed frequently for the public. Choral activities expanded after 1902, when the school relocated to Mount Auburn. Since the new campus included its own concert hall, public performances of choral programs became much easier to schedule.

In 1888 Clara Baur was invited to sponsor a Christmas program at her Conservatory that would feature the boys' choir of Camp Washington's Church of the Sacred Heart. The group was led by organist and choirmaster Harold Beckett Gibbs, who also headed the Conservatory's organ department. Only after 1902, however, was Baur able to present the type of Christmas program that would develop into the Feast of Carols, which still forms a well-loved part of CCM's roster of public offerings.

"[In] the architecture of the building at Oak Street and Highland [Baur found] an ideal setting for the singing of Christmas carols. The spacious hall of the house lent itself well to the entertainment of the limited number of guests then involved in the celebration. Seated in the hallway, guests could observe the lofty ceiling, the arched

flight of stairs leading to the balcony."[33]

The broad, ornately carved staircase and the airy entrance hall of the Shillito mansion were decorated with evergreen boughs, candles, and other ornaments to provide a picturesque setting for the program. This "Afternoon of Carols," given in January 1909, was so well received that it came to be presented annually.

The program of 1912 became the prototype for future presentations.[34] "Three tiny tots standing in the balcony opened the program with 'Long Ago,' and a small chorus of girls [probably Conservatory students, hence no longer 'girls'] gave charmingly a group of carols from the first balcony." A boys' choir, carrying lighted candles, proceeded down the staircase, singing the carol "Adeste Fidelis," then delivered several more carols. "Soon voices were heard from outdoors—the Wassailers—who entered through the main door and performed a group of carols." After several more selections, sung by Conservatory or invited groups, the boys' choir "departed as they had come.... It was for this program that Dr. [Harold Beckett] Gibbs coined the phrase 'Annual Feast of Carols,' which is still used. The Carols became a yearly Christmas festivity and were eagerly attended by many music lovers."[35]

Clara Baur founded the Cincinnati Conservatory in 1867 and served as its head until her death in 1912.

Feast of Carols Finale, December 2008. (Courtesy of Curt Whitacre)

Audiences for this celebration soon outstripped the space available to seat them, and in 1926 the Feast of Carols was moved to the Conservatory's concert hall. This hall not only provided for more spectacle but allowed larger and more varied performance forces as well. A description of the 1934 Feast of Carols, now directed by John A. Hoffman, speaks of a chorus of twenty-eight voices on stage, a similar chorus in the balcony, and an eight-piece string ensemble. The Conservatory-sponsored Boy Choristers Guild, a 22-voice group made up of children from the community and from faculty director Parvin Titus's Christ Church Cathedral, also participated. The program consisted of carols from alternating choruses, vocal solos, audience sing-alongs, and a massed finale on Gustav Holst's carol medley "Christmas Day." Other Feasts of Carols supplemented Conservatory forces with children's choruses drawn from various Cincinnati venues. In 1938, for example, the program featured a 175-voice chorus from Clifton School and the Twenty-third District School. In 1939 the program, having once again outgrown its performing space, was moved downtown to the Hall of Mirrors in the Netherland Plaza Hotel, where it remained for many years.

If the 1930s were bright years for the Feast of Carols, the 1940s required some cutbacks. The number of male students at the Conservatory declined greatly as America raised armies to fight in Europe and the Pacific. By 1950, however, performers at the Feast of Carols included a 55-voice Conservatory Concert Choir of mixed voices, a group of 112 children from Hyde Park School,

and Conservatory instrumentalists. In 1955, when the Conservatory and the College of Music merged, the additional students meant an even healthier choral program, and CCM's relocation to the University of Cincinnati campus in 1967 allowed the still popular Feast of Carols a new, permanent place in the new building's Corbett Auditorium.

The Chorus in the Curriculum

Though the Feast of Carols was surely the most consistently attractive offering of the Conservatory's Chorus, this group became both more and less than a performing group. Both Clara Baur and her niece and successor as Dean, Bertha Baur, considered the chorus to be first and foremost a vehicle for building musicianship, and a strong statement to that effect appeared yearly in catalogues of the early decades of the twentieth century.

"[The Conservatory aims] to make schooled musicians of its pupils. The thorough training of the ear and the sense of rhythm is the first requisite, and the best means to that end is long experience in chorus singing under a competent drill master. The importance of this cannot be easily overestimated, since there does not exist a musician worthy of the name, whether vocalist or instrumentalist, who cannot sing [in an ensemble] with ease and correctness. The Conservatory must, therefore, refuse either testimonial or certificate of any kind to those who have not attended the chorus rehearsals and made themselves proficient in this indisputable qualification of a musician."[36]

Later versions of this statement might be somewhat milder, but its purpose remained: the Conservatory Chorus was deemed an important

vehicle to make music students into finely developed musicians.

As a performing group, the chorus appeared under the able leadership of Harold Beckett Gibbs, who conducted such works as the cantata "King René's Daughter" by Henry Smart, Gounod's "Gallia," or Hummel's "Queen of the Sea," all fairly recent additions to the choral repertoire. Gibbs also used the Conservatory as a performance venue for the men and boys' choir he led at Cincinnati's Church of the Sacred Heart. He became well known for lecture-recitals on church music, especially Gregorian chant, and for concerts illustrating the history of church music, beginning with chant and ending with works of the later nineteenth and early twentieth century— perhaps a Mass by Rheinberger or Frank Van der Stucken's "Pax triumphans." In addition, Conservatory students often augmented the May Festival Chorus or, after 1920, took chorus roles in Cincinnati's Opera at the Zoo under Conservatory professor Ralph Lyford.

World War I affected the Conservatory Chorus in that many male members left school to join America's military forces. Women's choruses carried on during the school year and in the increasingly popular Summer Sessions. Along with Vincent d'Indy's "Saint Mary Magdalene," the women impressed local

a student's musical education was reaffirmed by a division of forces into a Workshop Choir of 27 voices and a Concert Choir of 50. Conductor Luther Richman described the Workshop Choir's course as the study of "a wide variety of music . . . in order to help participating students in future professional duties,"[37] while the Concert Choir became the school's major performing group. Together with the Concert Choir the Workshop Choir performed Joseph Clokey's *When the Christ Child Came Down,* John Stainer's *Crucifixion,* and Charles Gounod's cantata *Gallia.* Independently, the Concert Choir appeared in *The Rape of the Moon,* a cantata by William S. Naylor, and Charles Vardell, Jr.'s *The Inimitable Lovers.*

But the time of serious merger talks was also close at hand. In a symbolic meeting of 1954 the choruses of the Conservatory and the College of Music joined in a May Festival performance of the American premiere of Franz Schmidt's oratorio *The Book with Seven Seals* and the second American performance of Orff's *Carmina Burana.* In 1955 the two schools became one, the College-Conservatory of Music (CCM), and the College moved its students and faculty to the Mount Auburn campus.

horal Music at the College of Music of Cincinnati

The origins of Cincinnati's College of Music were far different from those of the Conservatory, with closer connections to the city's business community and its extant musical institutions.[38] Unlike the privately

Pictures from left to right: Elm Street Panorama: Memorial Hall, College of Music (two buildings), and Music Hall. Dexter Hall, first location of the College of Music. Conservatory of Music's entrance hall, site of the earliest Feasts of Carols.

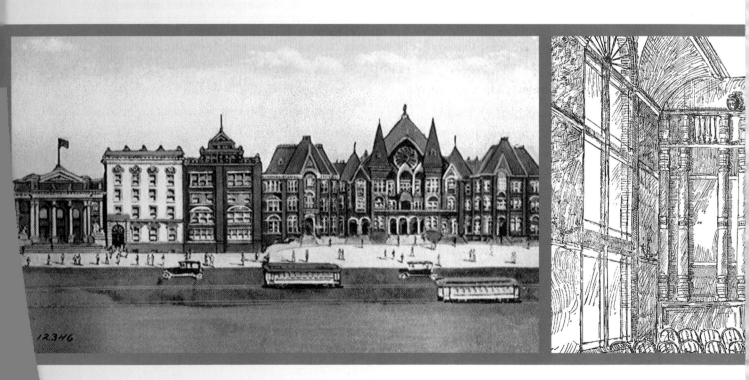

owned and operated Conservatory, the College was from its beginning in 1878 a corporation with a president, a board of trustees, and stockholders who actually expected no profits from their investment. In a letter George Ward Nichols, a principal stockholder, described the future college as "the centerpiece of a grand scheme to put Cincinnati at the center of the American musical universe."[39] And the College did in fact play its part as a strong participant in the string of new musical institutions that included the first May Festival (1873), the opening of Music Hall (1878), and the founding of the Cincinnati Symphony (1895). It would also find a place in the city's technological history when it developed the first college-based school of radio broadcasting (1936), which would expand to include the new medium of television and support the nation's first educational television station, WCET (1954). Because of the close connections established between the College's broadcasting division and Cincinnati's important clear channel station WLW, College performers, including its choral groups, were heard across the land.

Unlike Clara Baur, who found a permanent home for her Conservatory only in 1902, the founders of the College settled immediately into the first of its multi-building quarters. To Dexter Hall (now Corbett Tower), the third floor of Music Hall, would be added the Odeon, right next door, which provided the College its own concert hall, another classroom building, and a women's dormitory, all on Elm Street. The final building, on Central Parkway, is the only one still standing.

In their invitation to the noted conductor Theodore Thomas to be the College's leader, the founders clearly stated their purpose.

"It is proposed to establish an institution for musical education upon the scale of the most important of those of similar character in Europe, to employ the highest class of

professors, to organize a full orchestra with a school for orchestra and chorus, and to give concerts."[40]

During its first year the College did indeed give concerts involving orchestra and chorus, both ensembles under Thomas's direction, and Cincinnatians flocked to hear a Bach cantata, Rossini's *Stabat Mater*, or Schubert's Psalm 23.

In 1878 Theodore Thomas's reputation as a musician and musical leader was sterling. Some time before, he had founded his own orchestra and taken it on several tours of the country, bringing classical music to many who had seldom if ever heard an orchestra. Soloists often traveled with the group, among them the Cincinnati-born pianist Julie Rivé-King, whose mother, Caroline Rivé, had been Clara Baur's only singing teacher and served on the first Conservatory faculty. Though the College enrolled some three hundred day and evening students by the end of its first year, the forces needed for the Thomas-led concerts surely included members of his own orchestra and

Odeon Auditorium, College of Music of Cincinnati.

the city's established singing societies as well. In later years it was common for members of the Cincinnati Symphony to fill out sections of the College orchestra, and the chorus's evening rehearsals encouraged members of the community to join the group. This was still true some ten years later, when choral director B. W. Foley, with the help of Cincinnati's Apollo Club, formed a chorus of 150 for a series of three concerts. The sixty-piece orchestra included advanced students, members of the College's faculty, and the leading players from the city's Philharmonic Orchestra, a predecessor of the Cincinnati Symphony.

Theodore Thomas began his tenure at the College with enthusiasm, but policy differences with George Ward Nichols soon became insurmountable. In 1880 Thomas resigned, the newly formed College orchestra was temporarily discontinued, and the Board of Trustees acquired, if only temporarily, a more hands-on administrative role. By the 1887-88 school year, when the student body numbered 650, the catalogue

Top: The University of Cincinnati Men's Glee Club, 1929-30 school year. Bottom: The UC Men's Glee Club, 1931-32 school year. (Courtesy of *The Cincinnatian*)

Top: The UC Girls' Glee Club, 1929-30 school year.
Bottom: The UC Girls' Glee Club, 1931-32 school year, with director Sherwood Kains. (Courtesy of *The Cincinnatian*)

Threshold; and in 1941 the Club presented a program of Mendelssohn's *First Walpurgis Night* and selected operatic ensembles. In the School Music department Elizabeth Medert Taylor regularly led members of her conducting class in public performances.

Over the years the College of Music developed its own version of the Conservatory's Feast of Carols. At times these Christmas Musicales consisted largely of carols and Christmas motets, but larger works like Clokey's *When the Christ Child Came*, Saint-Saëns's *Christmas Oratorio*, Bach's *Christmas Oratorio*, Finzi's *Dies Natalis*, Schütz's *Christmas Story*, Britten's *Saint Nicholas*, or Bach's *Magnificat* might also be programmed.

In 1946 a new vocal ensemble was founded: the Quintones. At first only a quintet, by 1948 the group had added eleven voices and renamed itself the Silhouettes. Directed by Harold Anderson, they performed primarily at social and civic gatherings around town, delivering show tunes along with more classical choral repertoire. In 1951 the ensemble brought its show tune repertoire to the Music Hall stage for a Cincinnati Pops concert.

Also new in the 1940s was conductor Roland Johnson, a graduate of the College, who revived the strong choral presence at his alma mater. In the *Clarion* of October 1947 he announced an ambitious program involving a 150-voice chorus, a select choir of 40 voices, and a 24-voice women's choir. Though pictorial evidence does not support these figures, the years under Johnson's directorship and that of his successor, William Byrd, featured challenging repertoire, largely with orchestral accompaniment. Brahms's *Schicksalslied*,

Britten's *Festival Te Deum*, Ives's *Psalm 67*, Dumler's *Missa Gloria Dei*, Haydn's *Creation*, Mozart's *Mass in C Major*, Schütz's *German Magnificat*, Vaughan Williams's *Serenade to Music*, Stravinsky's *Symphony of Psalms*, Handel's *Messiah*, Fauré's *Requiem*, and faculty composer Jack Labunski's *There Is No Death* are typical examples. In addition, the College Chorus joined the Conservatory Chorus and other forces in performances of Mahler's Symphony No. 2, Orff's *Carmina Burana*, Cohon's *Let There be Light*, and other major offerings. But declining enrollments and attendant financial problems made the 1955 merger with the Conservatory all but inevitable. The College's doors closed at the end of the 1954-55 school year, and its students joined those of the Conservatory at the campus atop Mount Auburn.

Interlude: Choral Music on the University of Cincinnati Campus

Both the College of Music and the Conservatory had forged ties with the University of Cincinnati in the 1920s, when the demand for music teachers in public and parochial schools in Cincinnati and across the United States prompted the establishment of baccalaureate programs in School Music.[43] In the 1920s, Cincinnati's two major music schools set up cooperative programs with the University that admitted their students to general education and methods courses through the University's Teachers College. Graduate programs leading to Master's and Doctoral degrees in education with a music emphasis also became available, and were situated in the College of Education until

1962, when the College-Conservatory of Music became a formal part of the University.

For many years before the merger the University of Cincinnati (UC) maintained its own choral, instrumental, and theatrical activities, which were often led by faculty members from the Conservatory or the College. Student theatre troupes regularly presented plays, musicals, operettas, and student-authored revues, and the Bearcat Marching Band, ever-present at UC football games, became one of the largest and most admired bands in the nation. Campus instrumental ensembles also included a student orchestra (founded in 1925), the ROTC band, and a "Ukestra" for players of ukulele, guitar, banjo, mandolin, and the like. Choral organizations included the Men's and Women's Glee Clubs, the mixed-voice Schola Cantorum, the University Singers, a Men's Octet, and the Melody Club of the School of

Nursing. In the decades between the World Wars UC also sponsored a Music Club, which presented lectures and recitals by speakers and performers from the Conservatory or the College. These programs were intended to "interpret and explain some phase of their art" to student audiences who wished "to become better acquainted with the classics in music."[44]

The largest and longest-lasting of the choral organizations were the glee clubs, which were most often conducted by faculty members from the Conservatory. The oldest of these, the Men's Glee Club, was founded in 1920 and averaged 65-70 members. Its companion organization, the Girls' (occasionally, Women's) Glee Club, soon followed and averaged 55-60 singers. Both groups were active performers, appearing singly or in tandem in their regularly scheduled Fall and Spring concerts and at various campus and city functions. In 1923, for example, both groups sang for the Women's

Club of Cincinnati and on tour at Ohio State and Miami Universities.[45] Radio broadcasts would become regular activities for both groups, as would appearances at intercollegiate choral competitions. In 1931 the Glee Clubs, along with the University Orchestra, the Band, Varsity and Brass Quartets, and several soloists presented a "Benefit Musical Program Given by University Musical Organizations for the City's Unemployed" in Emery Auditorium. They raised some $500 for the city's Welfare Department.[46]

Today it may seem strange that a university in a city with a sizeable African-American population should exclude black students from so many social and extra-curricular activities. However, photos in the student yearbook, *The Cincinnatian,* clearly reveal the separation of races that prevailed on campus well into the twentieth century. Given the university's increasing activity in choral music in the 1920s and '30s, it is not surprising that a group of African-American women should form an ensemble of their own, the University Singers, in 1930. Male singers joined the group the following year, when it was renamed the University Singers and Players. Even after the College-Conservatory of Music joined other colleges at UC, the University Singers, now a 16-voice ensemble, continued to perform music from madrigals to modern tunes. Gradually all choral groups on campus and in CCM became integrated. In the 1970s the formerly all-black University Singers would be transformed into CCM's very popular show choir in which talent, not race, determined membership. Under the leadership of Earl Rivers the group's

Picture opposite page: The University Singers, 1930-31 school year. Below: The Melody Club, 1929-30 school year. (Courtesy of *The Cincinnatian*)

The original Mary Emery Hall
(1967), first on-campus home of the
College-Conservatory of Music, viewed from
the footbridge to Tangeman University Center.
(Courtesy of Cincinnati Historical Society)

performances of popular tunes, show medleys, even collections of television's best singing commercials, drew enthusiastic audiences from campus and city alike. This ensemble was discontinued in 1985.

On the other side of campus, women of UC's School of Nursing and Health came together in the fall of 1924 to form the Melody Club, a choral group with an average membership of 35-40 voices and the purpose of "fostering of musical interests and appreciation among the students and production annually of a concert for the benefit of the Student Activities Fund."[47] The Melody Club first appeared during the Christmas season as carolers in the halls of what is now University Hospital, then began their series of spring concerts with an operetta, *India*, for which the Conservatory provided a director, Annette Fillmore. Under Garner Rowell the Melody Club grew to as many as 70 voices, but eventually it would diminish in size and sing primarily for its members' own "recreation and social diversion" in once-a-week get-togethers.[48]

Meanwhile, on the University of Cincinnati's Clifton campus, Robert Garretson, a professor of music education at CCM, had reorganized the university glee clubs into a single, very active group of some hundred voices governed by a Glee Club Board that planned both the performance schedule and social activities for the group. Glee Club performances included two full on-campus concerts, appearances at other campus and city events, television broadcasts, and an annual tour during the break between winter and spring quarters. The University

Singers and Male Octet took part in many of these events. New on the schedule was the Glee Club's appearance with the Cincinnati Symphony Orchestra.

Though CCM would not be a physical presence on campus until 1967, it had become an official part of UC in 1962. Between 1955, when the merger of the College and the Conservatory had been effected, and 1966 the new CCM remained in the Mount Auburn facilities, but had begun using such UC venues as the Wilson and Annie Laws Auditoriums for some performances. The school year 1966-67 was a difficult one, for the CCM campus had been sold and had to be turned over to its purchaser—the Cincinnati Board of Education—before its new quarters at UC were ready. Yet choral and orchestral ensembles continued their normal activities in whatever campus facilities were available.

Permanent Home for CCM

"UC's New College-Conservatory of Music Is A Marvel of Engineering For The Musical Arts." So read the headline in the *Sunday Pictorial Enquirer,* a component of the *Cincinnati Enquirer,* on November 26, 1967. The cover photo featured the new building's Corbett Auditorium stage, on which were arranged the school's orchestra and one of its several choruses. Built largely with funds donated by Cincinnatians J. Ralph and Patricia Corbett, together with other local patrons of the arts, the new building represented the joining of the city's internationally celebrated music school and the university it had built and nurtured over the preceding one hundred years. The dedication celebration also marked the hundredth anniversary of the founding of the Cincinnati Conservatory by Clara Baur in 1867, and its programs featured triumphant appearances of the school's choral forces.

The largest production of the week— in fact, "one of the most elaborate and costly opera productions ever given in Cincinnati"[49]—was Borodin's *Prince Igor*. It filled the capacious stage of the 800-seat Corbett Auditorium with a cast of distinguished soloists, 40 dancers, and a 100-voice chorus trained by Elmer Thomas. An orchestra of some 90 players filled the pit, and all forces were led by conductor Erich Kunzel. On another festal program, CCM choruses presented premieres of two newly commissioned works: Norman Dello Joio's *Proud Music of the Stars*, by the 190-voice Choral Union, brass choir, and organ; and faculty composer Scott Huston's cantata *The Path and the Praise* by the 45-voice CCM Chorale, accompanied by the student orchestra.

Reactions to the performances and the new facilities appeared in newspapers and journals across the country. Perhaps the St. Louis *Post Dispatch* best summed up their significance: "It is reasonable to assume...that the Corbett Center for the Performing Arts and the College-Conservatory in general owe some of their vitality to the whole community."[50] And indeed, the choruses of the College-Conservatory of Music, along with those of the University of Cincinnati, had been a continuing musical presence in the city. Performances for community groups, religious

associations, and conventions continued to be common, as did appearances on the Cincinnati Symphony Orchestra's regular and Pops seasons and participation in the formerly biennial, now annual May Festival. In addition, CCM faculty members had frequently served as chorus masters of the May Festival Chorus and continued to do so: Elmer Thomas held this position from 1970 to 1975, and John Leman served from 1979 to 1988.

The still popular Feast of Carols continued to draw capacity audiences every year. Having been staged for many years in the Hall of Mirrors at the downtown Netherland Plaza Hotel, by 1965 this event had been moved to Wilson Auditorium on the University of Cincinnati campus. In 1967 it would find a new home in Corbett Auditorium, where it would continue to invite choirs from city and suburban schools or children's choirs from CCM's own Preparatory Division to join in the celebration. Finally, no better example of the school's community ties could be cited than that its new home on the university campus came into being on a foundation of private donations. The final piece of the performing arts complex, built with $5 million from the Corbetts, would be dedicated in 1972. This wing, the Patricia Corbett Pavilion, contained dance studios, classrooms, and the 250-seat Patricia Corbett Theater. When in 1977 Cincinnati's city university joined Ohio's state university system, all the physical and administrative pieces were in place; developments would

Exterior of Patricia Corbett Center, part of the CCM Village, containing the Patricia Corbett Theater, classrooms, offices, and dance studios. (Courtesy of Frank Pendle)

continue within the school itself.

Once settled in its new quarters, the CCM choral department began to take advantage of the rehearsal halls and performance areas now available to its students, and to work with the choral groups long in place at the university itself. Within ten years these ensembles ranged from the eight-voice Renaissance Consort to the larger Chorale and Motet Choir. The University Singers had been restructured as a show choir under the direction of Earl Rivers, assisted by choreographers Stephanie Rivers and, later, Joan Walton. Students from outside CCM were served by the traditional glee clubs, which would come under the management of CCM. In subsequent years the number and nature of the choral groups would change, but the opportunities available to students would grow and become more varied.

Even before CCM's move to the UC campus, plans were being made for Master of Music and Doctor of Musical Arts degree programs in both choral and orchestral conducting. These were finalized in 1968 and ensured that Cincinnati's reputation for both study and performance of choral music would increase over the final decades of the twentieth century and into the twenty-first. Students admitted to these programs gained experience leading some of CCM's

THEATER

standing ensembles or assisting faculty conductors in the preparation of the larger choral works scheduled during each season. Analysis and historical study were never far from performance, nor was performance far from the student body as a whole. Student singers welcomed opportunities to sing choral literature as they rehearsed for major concerts, or to serve as soloists in the oratorio repertoire necessary for a well-rounded career. Instrumentalists gained experience playing this literature as preparation for future jobs in America's orchestras. Because of the growth of the graduate conducting program, Cincinnati's churches and community choruses found CCM increasingly able to provide them with conductors, who in turn gained valuable experience as leaders of these ensembles.

By the 1970s, CCM, with its state-of-the-art physical facilities and the expanded possibilities these facilities brought for choral activities, performances, and advanced studies, could stand proudly next to established models provided by such metropolitan institutions as the May Festival, the Cincinnati Symphony Orchestra, the Cincinnati Opera, the newly founded Cincinnati Chamber Orchestra, and the growing number of suburban arts organizations, independent professional

and amateur groups for adults and children, and the performing arts educational institutions for children of all ages. City and campus activities brought new and exciting possibilities for choral music to the entire metropolitan area of Cincinnati.

Examples of this synthesis and growth can be found in CCM's contributions in two areas of Cincinnati's choral music scene: performance of major choral works of the past, and presentation of new works by living composers. The relocated, newly settled College-Conservatory of Music, with its large number and variety of choral groups, still performed on the regular seasons of the Cincinnati Symphony Orchestra and in the May Festival, doing such works as the Symphony No. 9 and *Choral Fantasy* of Beethoven, Bach's *Saint Matthew Passion,* Mahler's Symphonies Nos. 2 and 8, and Requiems by Verdi, Berlioz, or Brahms, working with the May Festival Chorus or with groups from nearby colleges, the Cincinnati Boychoir, the children's choirs of CCM or the city's School for Creative and Performing Arts (SCPA). On campus, CCM student forces presented similar choral-orchestral works, such as Mozart's Masses or his Requiem, Handel's *Messiah* with the original instrumentation, Stravinsky's *Symphony of Psalms*, both sets of Brahms's *Liebeslieder Waltzes*, Bruckner's *Te Deum* and Mass in Eb, Mendelssohn's *Elijah*, and Monteverdi's *Vespers of 1610*. In addition, CCM sponsored groups small enough to offer programs of Renaissance madrigals, chansons, or motets (Renaissance Consort), or specialized enough to present choreographed programs of show

tunes (University Singers), all traditional masterworks in their own right.

Both city and campus gave Cincinnati audiences the best in contemporary choral music as well. CCM singers joined the May Festival Chorus in Britten's *War Requiem* and Bernstein's *Mass*, performed Menotti's *The Unicorn, the Gorgon, and the Manticore* with the Cincinnati Symphony, and joined the Cincinnati Ballet for Orff's *Carmina Burana*. At CCM, choirs continued the traditions of both the Conservatory and the College by commissioning works from its faculty composers: for example, Paul Cooper's *Credo*, Norman Dinerstein's *Frogs*, Darrell Handel's *A Candle A Saint*, and several pieces by Scott Huston. Short works by Ives, Poulenc, Schoenberg, or Webern, Stravinsky's Mass and *Oedipus Rex*, Britten's Missa Brevis, the revised version of Carlisle Floyd's *The Martyr*, Ginastera's *Lamentations*, or Berio's Magnificat also found places on CCM programs. More recently, CCM forces have introduced Cincinnati to Philip Glass's Symphony No. 5, Penderecki's *Credo*, Tan Dun's *Water Passion*, and John Adams's *On the Transmigration of Souls*. Many conductors have been involved in these programs, from Lewis Whikehart, Elmer Thomas, and Douglas Amman, to John Leman, Earl Rivers, and Brett Scott. They have been assisted by many able students enrolled in the graduate programs in conducting. In these ways the choral singers of CCM have been able to give back to their campus and area-wide audiences the music that has won them the loyal and long-lasting critical and financial support of their community.

Top: Cincinnati Children's Choir's most advanced group, the Bel Canto Choir, with conductor Robyn Lana. Bottom: The CCM Chamber Choir, Chorale, Bel Canto Choir, Concert Orchestra, and student soloists, conducted by Earl Rivers, perform Philip Glass's Symphony No. 5 (2003). (Courtesy of Curt Whitacre)

The CCM Children's Choir

"It is the mission of the Cincinnati Children's Choir to offer children of all backgrounds the opportunity to experience musical excellence in a creative environment. Through performances together and in collaboration with professional ensembles and children's choirs throughout the world, the children demonstrate the knowledge gained, experience a sense of accomplishment, and cultivate greater self-esteem."[51]

To say that the Cincinnati Children's Choir is more than just a choir is not boasting—though there is much to boast about—but rather a recognition that it is a kind of choral system, providing a broadly based program of choral education and participation for children from grades 2-12 in the Greater Cincinnati-Northern Kentucky-Southeastern Indiana area who have usable voices and the will to sing. The Children's Choir bears the designation Ensemble-in-Residence at the College-Conservatory of Music (CCM). However, the group as a whole breaks down into six choirs whose members live within Greater Cincinnati plus an expanding system of five satellite choirs for children who live too far outside the central city to attend regular rehearsals on the university campus.

The Bel Canto Choir, the most advanced choir of those based at CCM, includes children from grades 6-12, plus some well qualified fifth graders, and is the group's main touring choir. The Girl Choir is made up of students from grades 10-12 who have fine vocal technique and music-reading skills. They perform with local professional ensembles and choirs from other areas of the country.

Pictures from left to right: The full array of Cincinnati Children's Choirs, led by Robyn Lana, performing in CCM's Corbett Auditorium (2009). The Bel Canto Choir on tour in Prague, 2004, with conductor Robyn Lana. The Festival Choir in an annual summer event. (Courtesy of Robyn Lana)

Their counterpart, the Young Men's Choir, is for boys and young men with changed or changing voices who participate in various activities of the total program and in outside events. Younger children may be placed in the Lyric Choir (grades 5-9) or the Jubilate Choir (grades 3-6). The youngest (grades 2-4) form the Preparatory Choir, where they receive training in note-reading, vocal technique, and solfege, and learn unison and two-part music. The newest of the satellite choirs meets at Miami University in Oxford; others meet in cooperating churches in Mason, Bridgetown, Batavia, and Lakeside Park, Kentucky. A sixth member will be added soon to the satellite choir roster when a group for children in grades 3-8 begins rehearsals at the University of Cincinnati's branch campus in Blue Ash. This choral web serves some 500 children from Greater Cincinnati and the surrounding area. Membership in all choirs is by audition.

To some extent the Cincinnati Children's Choir has built on the foundation of the CCM Children's Choir that was founded in 1983 by Karen Wolff, a member of CCM's Music Education faculty. Over the next decade, advanced choral conducting students and recent graduates of CCM assumed leadership of this group,[52] and the program was expanded to include its youngest children in a choir called the Mini-Singers. In 1993 Robyn Lana founded a separate choir, the Cincinnati Children's Choir, in affiliation with the city's Musical Arts Center. By 2001 the CCM Children's Choir merged with Lana's group and the united choirs became an Ensemble-in-Residence of CCM. As the choir's home base, CCM provides rehearsal and performance space, and the group reciprocates by taking part in the Conservatory's operas (e.g., Puccini's *Turandot*), larger choral-orchestral works (e.g., Glass's Symphony No. 5, Adams's *On the Transmigration of Souls*, J. S. Bach's *Saint Matthew Passion*, or

The Edgecliff Ensemble of Xavier University, a select group from Xavier's Concert Choir, with conductor Dr. Tom Merrill.

Orff's *Carmina Burana*), or the annual Feast of Carols. In addition, the Children's Choir has become a regular presence on programs of the Cincinnati Symphony Orchestra, the Kentucky Symphony Orchestra, the Vocal Arts Ensemble, and the May Festival Chorus, and can be heard on two recordings by the Cincinnati Pops.

By invitation the Cincinnati Children's Choir has performed before the Ohio Choral Directors Association and the American Choral Directors Association. Advanced singers have toured Canada, Ireland, Wales, Germany, Austria, the Czech Republic, England, and Scandinavia, and have sung at many American venues, often in collaboration with local children's choirs. In 2000 the group became one of the founding members of an international festival of children's choirs, Worldsong.

Robyn Lana, founder and artistic director of the Cincinnati Children's Choir, holds degrees in music education from the College-Conservatory of Music. She is a music specialist at the Montessori Academy of Cincinnati, and frequently appears as a clinician and guest conductor at meetings of professional choral directors' organizations. For the various subdivisions Children's Choir she has assembled a skilled staff of assistant conductors, often selected from among

Xavier University's Fall Choral Festival, held downtown at St. Xavier Church, Nov. 8, 2008, led by Dr. Merrill. The chorus includes Xavier's Concert Choir, St. Xavier High School Men's Choir, and the Women's Choir of the University of Cincinnati. (Courtesy of Dr. Merrill)

advanced students at CCM. Guided by these conductors, members of the Cincinnati Children's Choir enjoy not only challenging opportunities to perform but are involved in a broad, education-based program founded on methods established by such internationally respected music educators as Carl Orff, Zoltan Kodaly, Jacques Dalcroze, and Jerome Bruner. These singers learn healthy vocal production, sight-singing, music history and theory, and rehearsal techniques that lead to performances of high quality. Their repertoire is large and varied, and includes many pieces composed especially for them.[53] In all these ways, the Cincinnati Children's Choir seeks to turn its vision into reality:

"The Cincinnati Children's Choir will continue the rich cultural heritage of Cincinnati by enriching the children's lives through vocal artistry, musical experience, and self-pride while representing Cincinnati as youth ambassadors of its artistic future."[54]

Some Distinguished Others

Choruses have been part of the musical scene in Greater Cincinnati for some two centuries, which counts as a long time in so young a country as the United States. Among its institutions of higher education, the choral experience has often proved to be a drawing

Opposite page: Members of Northern Kentucky University's Vocal Jazz Ensemble. NKU's Chamber Choir with conductor Dr. Randy Pennington. This page: Views of NKU's Vocal Jazz Ensemble with Dr. Pennington. (Courtesy of Randy Pennington)

card in the educational packages offered to their students. Choral performances in turn have drawn attention and support from a listening public in a metropolitan area that stretches out on both sides of the Ohio River. Two very different institutions stand out: Xavier University (XU), a Jesuit-run school situated on rolling land on the east side of Cincinnati, and Northern Kentucky University (NKU), a relative newcomer to the area that occupies a growing campus high on a hill overlooking Highland Heights, Kentucky. Together, these institutions represent some of the best and most consistent developments on Greater Cincinnati's choral scene.

Xavier University is a private school of some 7,000 students distributed across 80 major fields.[55] Founded in 1831 as a men's college, it is the fourth oldest of America's Jesuit colleges and universities and the oldest university in Greater Cincinnati. Northern Kentucky University strongly contrasts with its Catholic neighbor in size and age.[56] Founded in 1968 as Northern Kentucky State College, it is the youngest comprehensive university in Kentucky's state system and in the Cincinnati metropolitan area. Its steadily growing student body now tops 15,000, and its expanding campus welcomed its latest addition, the College of Informatics, in 2006. Choral programs at both Xavier and NKU include many music majors but also draw on a full campus of undergraduate students from many other major fields to sing in their ensembles.

In the beginning, XU had no music department, though by the mid-nineteenth century it included at least one chorus among the extracurricular activities offered to students. Two important changes occurring in the twentieth century made choral music a more permanent part of campus life. The first came in 1969, when XU became a fully co-educational institution.[57] The second, in 1980, came in XU's decision to purchase nearby Edgecliff College, a Catholic school for women that offered courses in the fine arts, including art, music, and theater.[58] With Edgecliff came choral conductor and organist Helmut Roehrig, who headed the merged Xavier-Edgecliff music department until 1998 and helped establish choral music as a part of the curriculum.[59] By 1987 Edgecliff's academic departments had been moved to the main XU campus and the Edgecliff property was sold. In 2002 Dr. Tom Merrill became head of the XU music department and the school's principal conductor of choruses.

Today choral music is alive and well on the expanding XU campus. The music department sponsors four major ensembles: a Concert Choir of about 50 voices and the Edgecliff Ensemble, smaller group (16-24 voices) made up of selected members of the Concert Choir, both conducted by Dr. Merrill; a 40-voice Women's Chorus led by Music Education professor Linda Busarow; and a 20-voice Men's Chorus conducted by Robert Vance, a doctoral candidate in conducting at the University of Cincinnati. All groups include students majoring in music, but also draw from the ranks of those enrolled in other programs in XU's Arts and Sciences college. In addition, XU makes room for choruses without formal academic standing: a gospel choir, a show choir, and the Schola Cantorum. With the Concert Choir Dr. Merrill has programmed many major choral works, including Bach's *Magnificat,* Schubert's Mass in G, and Vaughan Williams's *Dona nobis pacem.* His efforts to move the choir outside its campus confines have resulted in performances of Orff's *Carmina Burana* with the Cincinnati Ballet and two appearances before meetings of the Ohio Music Education Association.

Like Tom Merrill, NKU's Randy Pennington aims to make his choirs part of moving his university out of its position as the area's best-kept secret. Proud of his school's accomplishments and its position as Kentucky's third-largest public university, Dr. Pennington has presented choirs of distinction and personality at a school where admission standards and visibility have risen consistently over the near-half century of its existence. Arriving in 1994, Dr. Pennington was only the third Director of Choral Studies in NKU's history. He has seen his area expand from two choirs to seven as the music department itself grew to some 180 majors, the largest percentage of them in the vocal area. The choirs, however, still draw on talent from the entire campus, as they have done throughout their history, giving over 250 students the opportunity to participate in a choral ensemble.

Dr. Pennington himself currently conducts two of the university's choirs: the Chamber Choir (a select ensemble of 32-36 voices) and the Vocal Jazz Ensemble (8-10 singers plus an instrumental combo). In addition to on-campus concerts, the Chamber Choir has appeared at various venues within Kentucky and, by invitation, at regional and national meetings of music education and choral directors associations. The group has also toured Great Britain and took a silver medal at the Busan International Choral Competition in South Korea. Likewise, the Vocal Jazz Ensemble has appeared at venues throughout southern Ohio and Kentucky, including Cincinnati's prestigious Blue Wisp Jazz Club and the Elmhurst Jazz Festival in Elmhurst, Illinois. Prof. Eric Knechtges, of NKU's theory and composition department, directs the New Music Ensemble, and adjunct faculty member Katie Barton leads the Northern Chorale and the 35-voice Women's Ensemble, NKU's newest chorus. The choral department also sponsors a Men's Choir and an Early Music Ensemble.

Greater Cincinnati's oldest and youngest universities are clearly making valuable contributions to the long tradition of choral performance that has distinguished the area for so many years. Joining them are the Athenaeum of Ohio, the College of Mount St. Joseph, the colleges and universities across southern Ohio, and the many public, private, religious, and charter schools from which future singers will come.

NOTES

1. School attendance for children ages 6-18 did not become mandatory until 1921.

2. Daniel Hurley, *Cincinnati, the Queen City* (Cincinnati: Cincinnati Historical Society, 1982), 55.

3. Walnut Hills High School moved to its current quarters on Victory Parkway in 1931.

4. "Cincinnati Independent Colored School System." http://www.ohiohistorycentral.org/entry.php?rec=856, accessed June 7, 2010.

5. G. F. Junkermann, Superintendent of Music, Cincinnati Public Schools, 1879-1900, writing in John Shotwell, *A History of the Schools of Cincinnati* (Cincinnati: School Life Co., 1902), 166.

6. Charles L. Gary, "A History of Music Education in the Cincinnati Public Schools" (EdD dissertation, University of Cincinnati, 1951), 210-21.

7. Ibid., 71-72.

8. Ibid., 212-13.

9. Ibid., 219-25.

10. Ibid., 211-12.

11. Ibid., 8-14. Much additional information for this section is based on Gary. Specific items will be noted separately as they arise.

12. G. F. Junkermann, cited in Constantine F. Soriano, "Cincinnati Music Readers" (MM thesis, University of Cincinnati, 1957), 56.

13. Revised and expanded, 1882; final revision, 1893. See Soriano, ibid., for further information.

14. Gary, "A History of Music Education," 223.

15. Walter M. Nicholes, "The Educational Development of Blacks in Cincinnati from 1800 to the Present" (EdD dissertation, University of Cincinnati, 1977), 104-13.

16. See Soriano, "Cincinnati Music Readers," 24, 79.

17. Gary, "A History of Music Education," 68.

18. Janelle Gelfand, "Hitting the High Notes with the Cincinnati Boychoir," *Cincinnati Enquirer*, April 30, 2010, E10.

19. Ibid.

20. Ibid.

21. For further information see http://www.cps-k12.org/schools/SchoolsChoice, accessed July 15, 2010.

22. *Newsweek* ranked it No. 66 in 2010, No. 43 in 2011; *U.S. News and World Report* judged it No. 88 in 2008, No. 36 in 2009, and No. 65 in 2010.

23. *Walnut Hills High School 2010-2011 Course Guide* (Cincinnati: Walnut Hills High School, [2010]). 4, 6.

24. Statistics from *U.S. News and World Report*, http://education.usnews.rankingsandreviews.com/best-high-schools/listings/ohio/walnut-hills/, accessed July 16, 2010.

25. *Walnut Hills High School 2010-2011 Course Guide*, 6.

26. Ibid.

27. Ibid., 29.

28. Winton Woods City Schools web page (http://www.wintonwoods.org/about-us/what-we-offer), accessed July 9, 2011, includes a list of courses and school activities offered at all grade levels in the district.

29. *YouTube* clips of Winton Woods High School choirs can be accessed via http://www.wintonwoods.org/schools/high-school/fine-arts/chorus and http://wintonwoodsacappella.webs.com/.

30. School for Creative and Performing Arts (SCPA) web page, http://www.scpak12.org/index.php/about/mission_and_vision_statement, accessed July 9, 2010.

31. Information for this section comes from Irving Brasch, "History of Secondary Education in the Parochial Schools of Hamilton County, Ohio" (MEd thesis, University of Cincinnati, 1938); Sr. Mary Joeline Ebertz, R.S.M., "A History of the Development of Music Education in the Archdiocese of Cincinnati" (EdD dissertation, University of Cincinnati, 1955); *Second Vatican Council*, http://mb-sort.com/believe/txs/secondvc.htm, accessed August 25, 2010; and *II Vatican Council—A Fulltext Search Engine of All Documents*, http://stjosef.at/council.search/, accessed August 25, 2010.

32. Information for this section is drawn from archival materials held by the University of Cincinnati Library's Archives and Rare Books Collection; and from Helen Board, *Bertha Baur: A Woman of Note* (Philadelphia: Dorrance & Co., 1971); B. J. Foreman, *College-Conservatory of Music 1867-1992: CCM 125*, ed Jerri Roberts ([Cincinnati:] University of Cincinnati, [1992]); John Lewis, "An Historical Study of the Origin and Development of the Cincinnati Conservatory of Music" (EdD dissertation, University of Cincinnati, 1943); William Osborne, *Music in Ohio* (Kent and London: Kent State University Press, 2004); and Lucinda Katheryne Travis, "A Study of the Vocal Programs at the Cincinnati Conservatory of Music, 1930-1950" (MM thesis, Cincinnati Conservatory of Music, 1950). Specific items will be cited separately.

33. Undated typescript (after 1948). Archives and Rare Books Collection, University of Cincinnati Library, UA-94-27, Box 2.

34. *Sharps and Flats* 5 #2 (March, 1914), 8.

35. Minna [Mrs. John A.] Hoffman, undated typescript. Archives and Rare Books Collection, University of Cincinnati Library, UA-94-27, Box 2.

36. Cincinnati Conservatory of Music, *Catalogue, 1920-21,* 24.

37 *A Tempo.* Yearbook of the Cincinnati Conservatory 1951, n. p.

38. Information for this section is drawn from archival material held by the University of Cincinnati Library's Archives and Rare Books Collection; B. J. Foreman, *College-Conservatory of Music 1867-1992: CCM 125*; William Osborne, *Music in Ohio*; Vincent A. Orlando, "An Historical Study of the Origin and Development of the College of Music of Cincinnati" (Ed.D. dissertation, University of Cincinnati, 1946); and Larry Wolz, "The College of Music of Cincinnati: A Centennial Tribute," *Bulletin of the Cincinnati Historical Society* 36 #2 (1978): 104-115 Specific items will be noted separately.

39. Foreman, *College-Conservatory of Music*, n.p.

40. Anonymous booklet, *College of Music of Cincinnati (1878-1955). 125th Anniversary Grand Celebration, October 16-17, 2003* (Cincinnati: n.p., n.d.).

41. By 1895 there were 800 students enrolled, taught by nearly 80 faculty members.

42. College of Music of Cincinnati, *College Bulletin for 1899-1900.*

43. Information for this section is drawn from archival material held by the University of Cincinnati Library's Archives and Rare Books Collection; William Osborne, *Music in Ohio*; and Mary Jo Souder, "The College Conservatory of Music of Cincinnati 1955-1962: A History" (MM thesis, University of Cincinnati, 1970). Specific items will be noted separately.

44. *The Cincinnatian* (Cincinnati: The Students of the University of Cincinnati, 1921), 131.

45. *The Cincinnatian* (Cincinnati: The Students of the University of Cincinnati, 1923), 179.

46. *The Cincinnatian* (Cincinnati: The Students of the University of Cincinnati, 1931), 149.

47. *The Cincinnatian* (Cincinnati: The Students of the University of Cincinnati, 1925), 106.

48. *The Cincinnatian* (Cincinnati: The Students of the University of Cincinnati, 1930), 322.

49. *Cincinnati Enquirer*, November 14, 1967.

50. *St. Louis Post Dispatch*, December 10, 1967.

51. The Cincinnati Children's Choir, Mission Statement, http://www.cincinnatichoir.org, accessed September 9, 2010.

52. These included Shirley Raut, Laurin Plant, Ann Marie Koukios, Robyn Lana, Christa Joy Chase, and Thomas Juneau.

53. A list of these pieces can be found on http://www.cincinnatichoir.org. Some performances are available on *YouTube*.

54. Ibid.

55. Information on Xavier University draws on Roger C. Fortin, *To See Great Wonders: A History of Xavier University 1831-2006* (Scranton, PA: University of Scranton Press, 2006); an interview with Dr. Tom Merrill, head of Xavier's music department; and the university's web site, http://www.xavier.edu, accessed September 1, 2010.

56. Information on Northern Kentucky University (NKU) comes from an interview with Dr. Randy Pennington, Director of Choral Activities at NKU; the university's web site, http://www.nku.edu, accessed September 1, 2010; and CD recordings of NKU choral ensembles.

57. Fortin, *To See Great Wonders*, 293-96. Shortly after the end of World War I the university began to admit women on a limited basis, as part-time students in evening and graduate programs.

58. Ibid., 295.

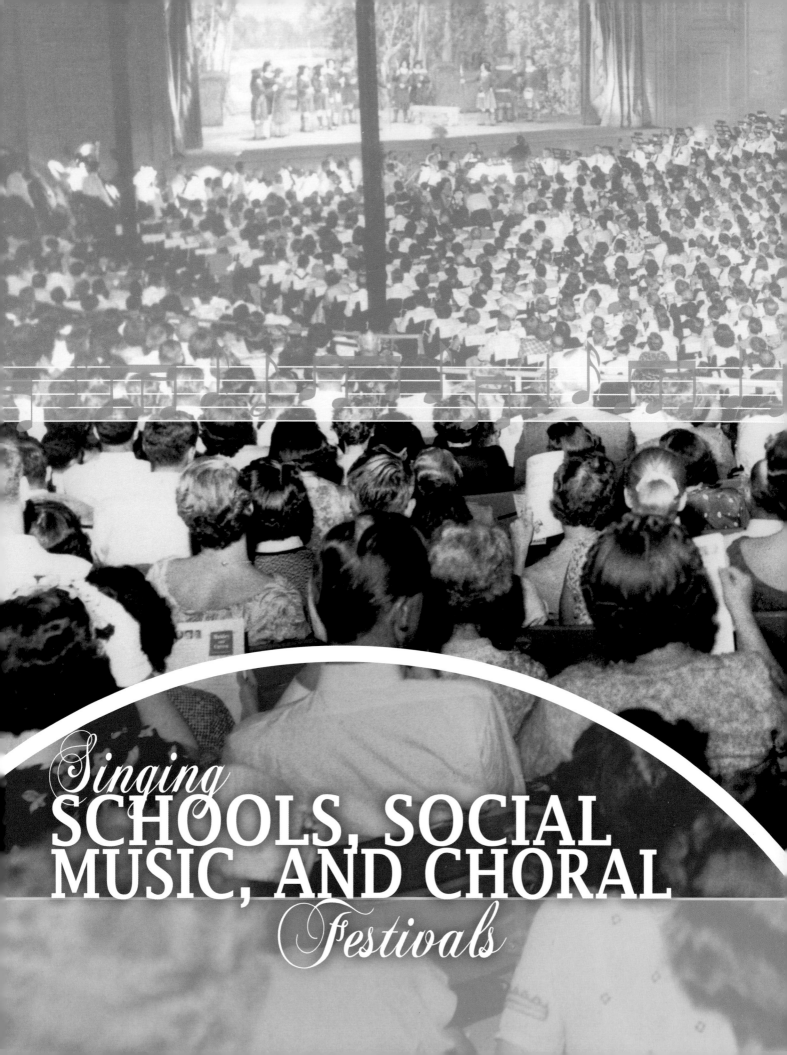

Singing
SCHOOLS, SOCIAL
MUSIC, AND CHORAL
Festivals

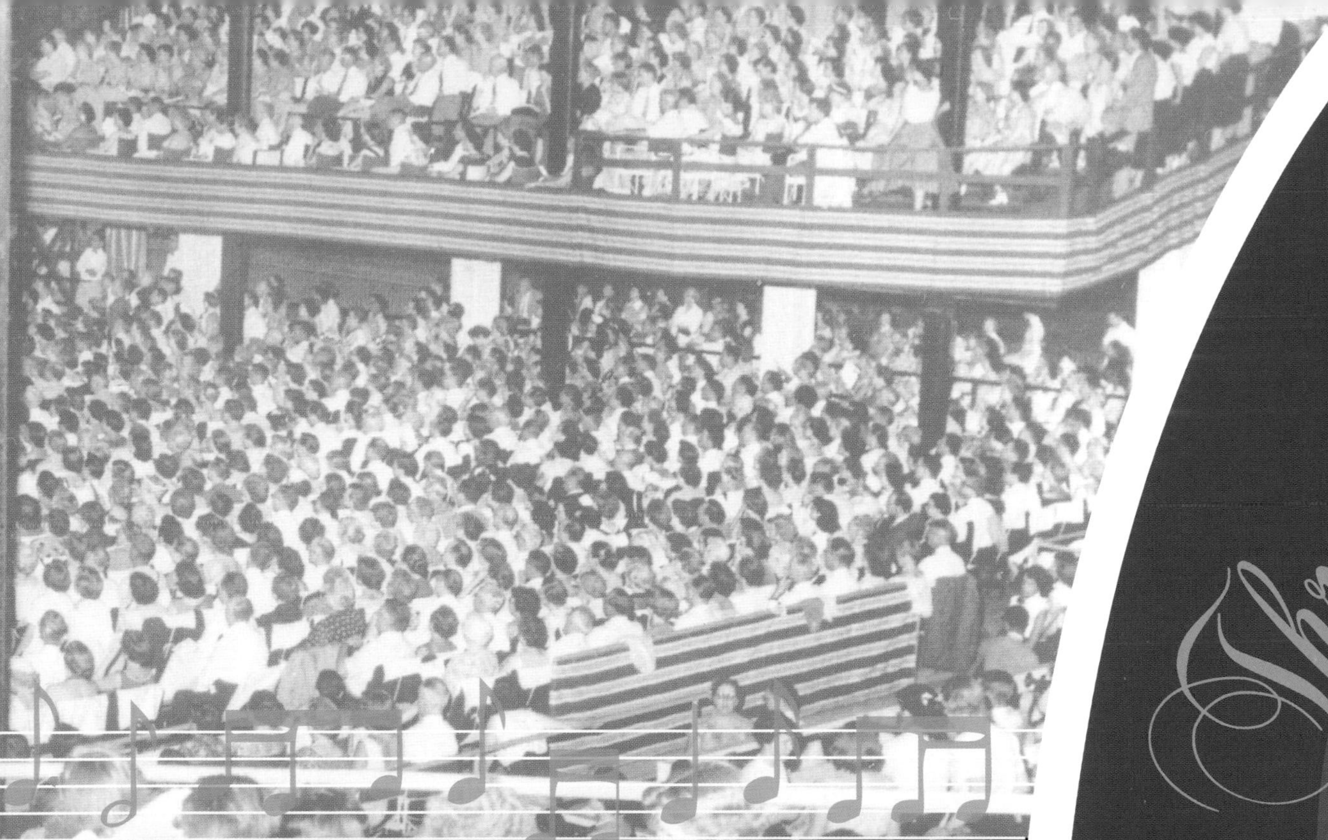

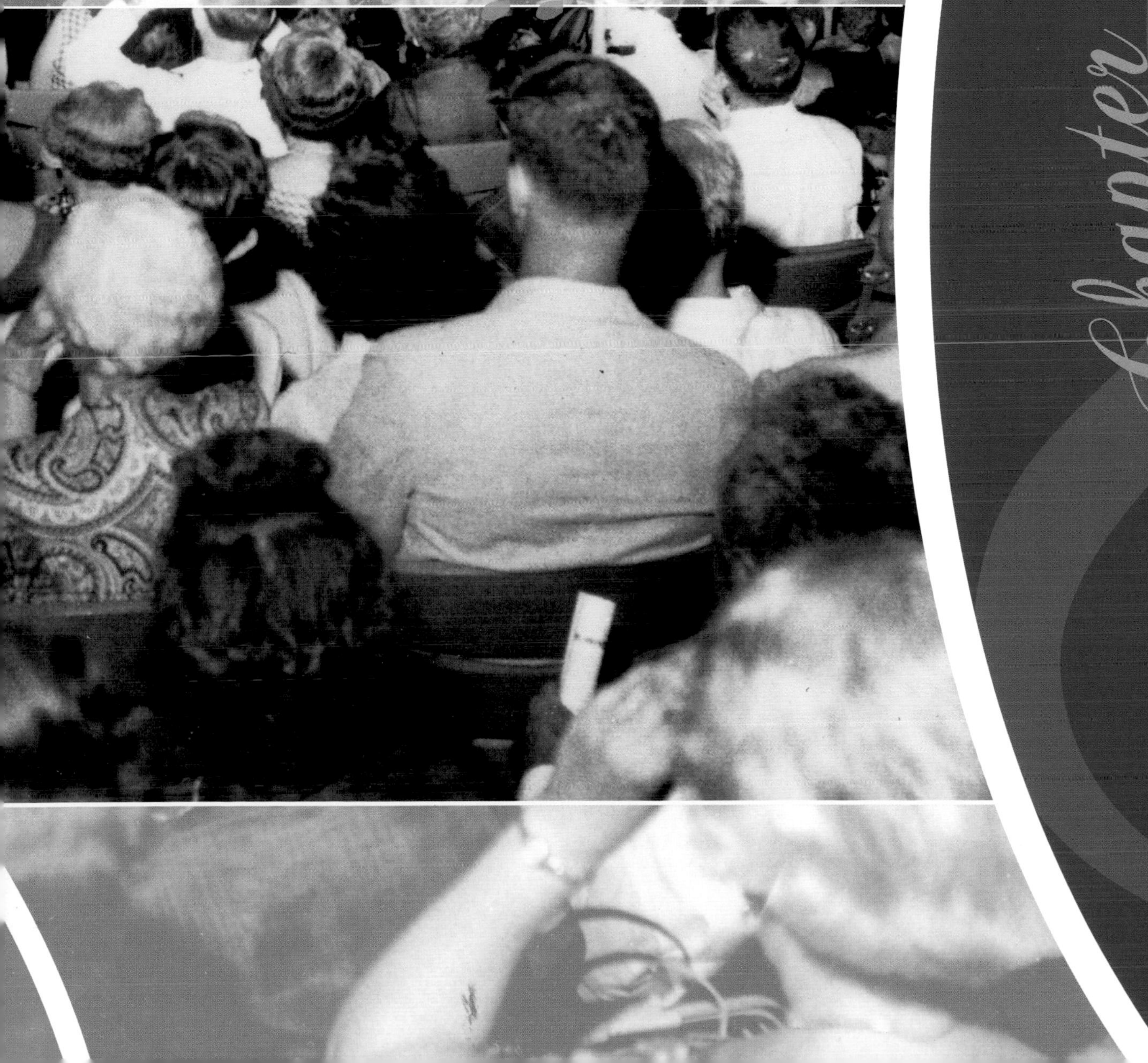

Chapter Three

by Craig Doolin

Cincinnati was founded in the first wave of expansion past the Allegheny Mountains. It was a western city that, like other settlements that gained notoriety—most notably Chicago and St. Louis—came of age only when it could vie with its eastern counterparts for dominance. This chapter examines how early attempts by Cincinnati citizens to become adequate singers in church and social situations led to the city's being recognized, by the late nineteenth century, as the most musical city in the United States. It further explores how the establishment of musical festivals in the 1800s enriched Cincinnati's artistic life in the twentieth century and beyond.

SINGING SCHOOLS

Cincinnati's musical beginnings appear almost as soon as the city was founded. In the America of Colonial times and well into the nineteenth century, singing schools represented the heart of musical instruction. These institutions first appeared in New England, where they trained pupils to be good congregational singers and provided further instruction for those who wished to pursue such studies. According to a retrospective account from 1888, Cincinnati's singing schools provided for social needs in addition to musical instruction.

They were sources of knowledge and places where study was most pleasantly combined with innocent, healthful social intercourse and mediums for the spread of musical knowledge—shall it be condemned because that knowledge was limited?—before the country had gathered sufficient abundance of wealth and leisure to attract a higher order of talent, or to enable well disposed students to seek further advantages abroad.[1]

In 1800, when the city was just a village of 750 people, the first singing school opened. The *Western Spy* published a notice in its December 17 edition that marked the founding of the first known singing school in the city's history:

"Those gentlemen and ladies who feel themselves disposed to organize a singing school will please to convene at the courthouse to-morrow evening at candle light, as it is proposed to have singing. Those who have books will please bring them."[2]

The following year a Mr. McLean, who operated a singing school but was also employed as a butcher, advertised his services. He offered a subscription price of one dollar for thirteen lessons or two dollars per quarter. For heat and light, students had to bring their own wood and candles.[3]

SINGING SOCIETIES

Cincinnati's tradition of singing societies is the foundation for choral music in the Queen City. In the mid-1810s the earliest societies paved the way for dozens of later groups and made possible the large festivals of the latter part of the century. Singing societies in Cincinnati during the nineteenth century belong to two traditions, commonly denoted as English and German. The nationalities attached to the choirs indicate not just the language of singing, but also the social framework of the meetings, especially within the German tradition. In reality, some of the founders of the English societies, particularly in the mid-nineteenth century, were of German heritage.

As a rule, the differences between the two national choral traditions were in language, origin, composition, and social scope. English societies, the earliest of Cincinnati's choral ensembles, existed primarily to make music. Many of these mixed choruses (usually SATB) grew from church choirs that invited outside singers to perform large works in concert, in addition to their liturgical duties. While every civic chorus provides social benefits to its members, those of the English tradition did not emphasize community. The first German society was founded in 1825, but the majority of these organizations arose after an immigration boom in the late 1840s. They provided social opportunities for eating and drinking, as well as making music. Most of the German societies were men's choruses, but women were sometimes admitted, often as non-singing supporting members, in the last half of the century. This section will trace the development of several of the more important societies of both traditions.

Much of the information about this period, especially regarding the German societies, comes from the 1912 recollections of Heinrich Rattermann (1832-1923). Not only was Rattermann the leading historian of the German-American community in Cincinnati, but he also founded the German Mutual Insurance Company that was housed in the iconic Germania Building in the then-booming business district of Over-the-Rhine.[4] Rattermann was a singer in the first Saengerfest (1849)

and was present at the initial meeting that resulted in the first May Festival in 1873.

THE ENGLISH TRADITION

he importance of the singing societies that existed in Cincinnati during the early nineteenth century is evident from the two important volumes of choral music published here during the decade. Both are in the shape-note tradition that has become known in recent years as Sacred Harp singing, named after a later publication.

German-born insurance magnate Heinrich A. Rattermann (1832-1923) moved to Cincinnati as a child. He sang in the 1849 Saengerfest and was involved in the early planning for the first May Festival in 1873.

John McCormick's *The Western Harmonist*, a collection of hymns and anthems, was advertised in *Liberty Hall* on April 8, 1815.[5] The following year, Timothy Flint published a similar volume, entitled *The Columbian Harmonist*, in Cincinnati. In his landmark *Centennial History of Cincinnati*, Charles Greve explains: "The demand for such works is mute evidence that there existed... singing bodies whose requirements made the publication of these song collections necessary."[6] Cincinnati would become an important center for music publishing in the later decades of the nineteenth century.

The Apollonian Society, first active about 1816, was the first of the early groups that has preserved information about membership. It met at 75 Sycamore Street, in the home of Frederick Amelung, a musician who assembled the group. Among its members were Cincinnati citizens from every walk of life, including dancing master Philibert Ratel, piano maker George Charters, pharmacist Edward Stall, confectioner Carl Ritter, and Martin Baum, the founder of the Western Museum who built the home that now serves as the Taft Museum. It was largely a group of amateurs who joined for pleasure. Little is known of another group, the Cecelia [sic] Society, except that it existed in 1816.[7]

In 1819 two important societies were born. The first of these was the Episcopal Singing Society, which first met at Christ Episcopal Church on Sixth Street. Arthur St. Clair, in 1788 the first governor of the Northwest Territory, provided the society the gift of a lot and Jacob Baymiller, a member of the Board of Directors of the Farmers and Mechanicks [sic] Bank and treasurer of the Sunday School Society of the Episcopal Church, paid for a house to be built for rehearsals. There is no indication that this society provided music for church services. By far the most important of the early societies was the Haydn Society, conducted by Philibert Ratel. This ensemble was unique in that it consisted of several smaller societies and combined church choirs. Coordinators of the Haydn Society were Edwin Mathews and Charles Fox, who operated a singing school at the Second Presbyterian Church on Walnut Street. The Haydn Society's first concert was a May 25, 1819, benefit to raise funds for a new organ for Christ Episcopal Church. Among the twelve choruses and anthems on the program were Haydn's "The Marvelous Work" from *The Creation* and Handel's "Hail Judea" from *Judas Maccabaeus*.[8] Later that year they held another benefit; this time half of the proceeds were earmarked for Sunday schools. Tickets sold for one dollar each.[9]

The early 1820s saw continued growth of Cincinnati's musical community. Charles Fox presented a joint concert of three combined singing societies on July 18, 1821. Although the identity of the participating societies has not been preserved, it is known that they sang excerpts from Handel's *Messiah* for the first time in the city. In 1822 the Harmonical Society rehearsed at the Miami Bank. The following year, the New Jerusalem Singing Society, an ensemble associated with the Swedenborgian church, rehearsed every Saturday night at the New Jerusalem Temple. Its leader, Adam Hurdus, was Cincinnati's first organ builder and also operated a dry goods store. On Sundays, he served as a pastor at the Temple. Also in 1823, the Euterpeian Society, a group whose performances were "seldom excelled this side of the Atlantic," presented a concert on July 18. On January 23, 1824, the Euterpeian Society gave a benefit concert for the Greek nation in their struggle against Turkish forces.[10]

Joseph Tosso, one of the most important names in instrumental music of the period, was the director of the orchestra of the Cincinnati Theatre. On February 23, 1832, he led chorus and orchestra in a concert for flood relief. Among the numbers performed were choruses from Handel's *Messiah* and Haydn's *The Creation*.[11]

Another major figure of the period, Victor Williams, was a well-rounded conductor of both choral and orchestral music. Swedish by birth, Williams had first lived on the east coast, but moved to Cincinnati in 1840 to join the faculty of the Eclectic Academy of Music. The same year, he became the director of the choir at the Ninth Street Baptist Church, a position that he held for fifty years. Using his church choir as the nucleus, he created the Sacred Music Society, a choir of 150 voices that presented concerts at various churches in the city. He founded the American Amateur Association, which provided orchestral accompaniment, in 1846.[12] Using members of the American Amateur Association and the Sacred Music Society, Williams led the

first complete performance of an oratorio in Cincinnati. The date of this performance is sometimes reported as 1840, but since the American Amateur Association was not yet founded, it must have taken place at a later time. This is supported by Heinrich Rattermann's 1912 recollection that the concert was held in Melodeon Hall, which was built in 1846, the same year that he immigrated to Cincinnati from Germany.[13] The American Amateur Association folded in 1853. In 1854, the Sacred Music Society sang with the Germania Musical Society, a touring 21-piece orchestra based in Boston and led by Carl Bergmann, an associate of Theodore Thomas. In 1873 Thomas would become the founding conductor of the May Festival. For the two Cincinnati concerts, Williams conducted Andreas Romberg's *The Power of Song* and Ferdinand Ries's *Der Morgen*. Although the Sacred Music Society was popular, its following waned over the years. During the Civil War, the Society withdrew from the public eye to concentrate on its role at the Ninth Street Baptist Church.[14]

Timothy B. Mason, organist at Lyman Beecher's Second Presbyterian Church and voice professor at the Eclectic Academy of Music, formed the Handel and Haydn Society in 1844. Although the group only existed for five years and never reached the level of expertise of the Sacred Music Society, it consisted of seventy-five singers and rehearsed at the New Jerusalem Temple on Longworth Street.[15] The Morris Chapel Singing Society, founded in the late 1840s, rehearsed at the Chapel on Central Avenue (then Western Row), between Fourth and Fifth Streets. Under the direction of Elisha Locke, the society of one hundred voices gave a performance of Haydn's *The Creation* at Melodeon Hall during the 1851-52 season. Their accompanist, Frederick Werner-Steinbrecher, was a piano-maker who had studied with Chopin.[16]

With the immigration of many Germans to Cincinnati during the 1840s and '50s, the story of choral music in Cincinnati begins to focus on their societies. However, the founding of the Apollo Club on January 3, 1883, was an attempt to bridge the deep division that had resulted between German, English, and a small number of Welsh choruses in the city. Starting with just twenty-two singers, the Apollo Club grew to an impressive fifty-six at the beginning of its sixth season. This mixed chorus performed in the best halls in the city – Smith and Nixon's Hall, the Odeon, Melodeon Hall, and Robinson's

Opera House. They assisted during the opera festivals in 1883-84 (see Chapter 2) and became a respected ensemble, performing in concerts as far away as Louisville, Kentucky. Fortunately, the programs of their first six seasons are preserved and show a diverse blend of works from composers such as George Frideric Handel, Felix Mendelssohn, Leo Delibes, and Hubert Parry. American composers George Whitefield Chadwick and John Knowles Paine are also represented.[17]

THE GERMAN TRADITION

Cincinnati is a melting pot of many cultures, but the Germans who immigrated to the city in the nineteenth century have shaped the city more than any other group. Even today, a hundred years after the German immigration

Pictures from left to right: Martin Baum, the fifth mayor of Cincinnati (1807), was a founding member of the Apollonian Society. The 1,200-seat Odeon was located in the College of Music adjoining Music Hall. Robinson's Opera House was one of the largest halls in Cincinnati with a capacity of 1,800. Between 1846 and 1867, Melodeon Hall stood on the northwest corner of Fourth and Walnut Streets.

THE
COLUMBIAN HARMONIST:
IN TWO PARTS.

TO WHICH IS PREFIXED
A DISSERTATION UPON THE TRUE TASTE IN CHURCH MUSIC,
BY
TIMOTHY FLINT, A. M.

CINCINNATI:
PUBLISHED BY COLEMAN AND PHILLIPS.
Looker, Palmer & Reynolds, Printers.
1816.

An example of shape notation from early 19th-century Cincinnati.

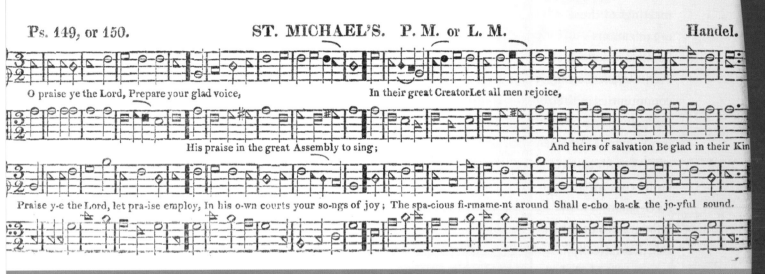

five years and two other directors stepped to the helm within the next four years. Finally, in 1873 Otto Singer, a prominent musician who would later create many piano-vocal scores of Wagner's operas, took over, but the chorus saw reduced membership and enthusiasm.

Another society, also called Germania, was formed in 1872 to honor Franz Abt, the German composer of many works for German male choruses. Conceived as an eight-person ensemble, Germania became the most honored society of its time. In 1883 it merged with the Maennerchor under the new moniker of Cincinnati Musik Verein and was led by Otto Singer until 1888, when Louis Ehrgott assumed leadership.[28]

One of the most important forces in unifying the German population in Cincinnati was the Turnverein, founded by German revolutionaries in 1848. These "Forty-Eighters" were political refugees from the failed Revolution of 1848, which had sought the unification of the German kingdoms. One of the leaders of this movement was Friedrich Hecker (1811-1881), who presented a unification resolution to the Frankfurt Preliminary Parliament in March of 1848. In April Hecker proclaimed the German Federation to be free and expected tens of thousands of people to join an army in defense of his cause, but only a few thousand were ready to oppose their current government. Hecker's movement was defeated and he left Germany in exile, moving first to Switzerland, then to London for a meeting with Karl Marx and Friedrich Engels, and on to New York. He reached Cincinnati late in the year. In November of 1848 Hecker and other refugees founded the Cincinnati

Turnverein, an organization dedicated to the importance of physical and intellectual well-being. This popular organization was very active in liberal politics, which at the time led them to support early Republican candidates. As the Turners spread throughout the Midwest, they bolstered German-American support for their cause and were instrumental in the election of Abraham Lincoln in 1860.[29]

In 1849 the Cincinnati Turnverein built a large hall at 1409-1413 Walnut Street in Over-the-Rhine. Turner Hall boasted all the amenities that supported their social, cultural, and political mission, best demonstrated by their motto of "Frisch, Fromm, Fröhlich, Frei" (Fresh, Virtuous, Happy, Free). The hall provided ample space for large physical education classes, along with studios for art instruction, a library, a German theater troupe, bands, and choruses. Many of the German singing societies met at Turner Hall and the Turner influence on Cincinnati's German immigrant society was profound.[30]

SAENGERFESTS

lthough the German singing societies were of great musical and social importance, they were small organizations. By the late 1840s, there arose a need for larger choruses, especially as a show of unity for the large influx of immigrants that flooded Cincinnati at the time. Rattermann described their dilemma:

"The narrow compass to which these societies, according to their nature and tendency, were limited, soon called for an extension of the boundary. This could not be accomplished in one association, as that would soon become unwieldy for the general purpose. The Liedertafel, as societies for the object of cultivating the male voice chorus, without instrumental accompaniment, are called, and of which the first was founded in Berlin under Zelter in 1809, are, on account of their original intention, not adapted for massive choruses. Wherever they are found, they seldom number as many as a hundred singers, generally averaging about twenty-five members. If then, a more powerful, a massive chorus is desired, it becomes necessary to bring several of these Liedertafel together, and by their united efforts the massive chorus is obtained. For that purpose festivals, to be given at stipulated intervals in the larger cities of a country, are devised. The earlier of these festivals had their origin in Germany. The first festival of the kind was held in the city of Wuerzburgh [sic], in Bavaria, August 4th to 6th, inclusive, 1845."[31]

During the first four days of June of 1849, just four years after the Würzburg festival, Cincinnati's Liedertafel, Schweitzer Gesangverein, and Gesang- und Bildungsverein joined with the Liederkranz of Louisville, Kentucky, and Gesangverein of Madison, Indiana, to create the Nord-Amerikanischer Saengerbund, an organization dedicated to establishing friendly ties through song. In total there were 118 singers, including Heinrich Rattermann. Conducted by William Runge, the inaugural concert on Friday, June 1, at Old Armory Hall on Court Street between Main and Walnut Streets, included music performed by each individual society, along with four selections by the "mass chorus of all associations." Composers represented on the program were largely those unique to repertoire of the German singing societies, including works by the now-unfamiliar Carl Frederick Zoellner, Konradin Kreutzer, Friedrich Silcher, and Franz Abt. The social highlight of the event was a picnic attended by several thousand people, during which the choruses provided informal entertainment.[32]

The Nord-Amerikanischer Saengerbund decided to make the Saengerfest an annual event and met every year until 1860. After the Civil War ended the Saengerfests resumed, but their frequency was somewhat erratic, occurring sometimes only every two or three years. This was likely because of the dramatic growth of the number of participants in these events, as demonstrated in Table 2 on page 116.

Cincinnati played an important role in the Nord-Amerikanischer Saengerbund by hosting six of their Saengerfests after the inaugural festival. The 1851 Saengerfest was held at College Hall in the Mercantile Building at the present site of the Mercantile Library on Walnut Street between Fourth and Fifth Streets. The 247-member chorus conducted by Robert T. Hoelterhoff and William Klausmeyer performed works by many of the same composers represented at the first festival. Newport, Kentucky's United States Military Band played Gioachino Rossini's

Built in only three months during the spring of 1899, the massive Jubilee Saengerfest Hall was not intended to last for decades. In fact, during the construction process it was deemed unsuitable, and portions had to be rebuilt. It opened a day late and at least two people were injured by falling timber. Although $40,000 was earmarked for the project, the actual cost approached $100,000. The cost overrun fell to the thirty-one members of the Board of Directors of the Jubilee Saengerfest as a personal debt. They paid a total of $67,000 to cover the labor costs, but they still remained over $30,000 in debt.[1]

Fearing that the remainder of the costs would also fall to them, the Board asserted that they had acted out of civic duty, and the remainder should be raised from the community. An appeal was sent to the public to raise $70,000—an amount that would reimburse the Board and defray legal fees. Unfortunately, the proceeds from this appeal only amounted to $1,800.[2] Next, the Board decided to distance themselves from the debt by incorporating a legal entity called "The Convention Hall Company," which would assume ownership of the hall and maintain it for future use. This was essentially a ploy to remove them from personal liability. They devised a plan to have a series of high-profile concerts in order to raise the deficient funds, but the Cincinnati Zoological Company, which owned the land upon which the hall was built, balked at the idea because they shared the legal liability for injuries.[3]

Recognizing the very real possibility of being stuck with ownership of a dangerous concert hall, the Board decided to sell tickets for a drawing that would give the winner the opportunity to buy Jubilee Saengerfest Hall for only $10,000. However, attorneys for the Board determined that this constituted a lottery, which was illegal according to state and federal law. As the Board became more desperate, they decided to sell the building at public auction for a starting bid of $5,200 after which the highest bidder would be required to move the hall to a new site within three months, but that plan never came to fruition.[4]

The Board made one final move. It hired the attorney Herman J. Witte to investigate the possibility of holding a high-profile sporting event in the hall. After some discussion, they settled on a boxing match. Witte went to New York to meet with representatives for "Gentleman" Jim Corbett and James J. Jeffries, both famous pugilists at the time. On December 8, 1900, it was decided that heavyweight champion Jeffries would face Gus Ruhlin, an Ohio boxer, in the ring at Jubilee Saengerfest Hall on February 15, 1901. Backed by "Boss" Cox, Mayor Julius Fleischmann supported the idea, but Governor George K. Nash claimed that the event was a prize fight, which was specifically outlawed in the state of Ohio. Local officials claimed that the proposed match was simply a fundraising event, since the boxers would be paid a lump sum, of which the winner would claim seventy-five percent. After much legal wrangling, Governor Nash called their bluff and pledged to send a thousand troops from the Sixth Ohio Regiment in Toledo to Jubilee Saengerfest Hall on the day of the proposed fight to prevent it from taking place.[5]

In the end, a landmark lawsuit (Ohio v. Hobart) ruled that the event was, in fact, a prize fight and disallowed it because state law supersedes local authority. Judge Howard Hollister issued a permanent injunction, after which Governor Nash stated that no prize fights would be allowed to occur on his watch. He used his influence to push through legislation that gave him limited veto authority.[6] The fight never happened, and Jubilee Saengerfest Hall was torn down in 1901.[7]

Jubilee Saengerfest Hall, built for the 1899 festival, stood on the site of a present-day parking lot for the Cincinnati Zoological and Botanical Gardens. Notice the patches on the roof and doors that appear to be sealed with boards. This hall was only two years old when it was razed in 1901.

1. Howard Clark Hollister, "The State of Ohio ex rel. J. M. Sheets, Att[orne]y Gen[era]l v. William N. Hobart, et al.," in *Ohio Misi Prius and General Term Reports: Ohio Courts of Common Pleas and Probate Courts of Ohio, Also of the Superior Court of Cincinnati at General and Special Terms 8* (Columbus: Weekly Law Bulletin, 1901), 247-248.
2. Ibid.
3. Ibid., 248.
4. Ibid.
5. Albert Shaw, "The Progress of the World," *in Review of Reviews and World's Work* 23, no. 3 (New York: Atlantic Monthly, 1901), 265.
6. Jeffrey T. Sammons, *Beyond the Ring: The Role of Boxing in American Society* (Champaign, IL: University of Illinois Press, 1990), 28.
7. Shaw, 265.

William Tell Overture and François Boieldieu's *Caliph of Baghdad* Overture, and ended the evening with a military march. Of the thirteen societies involved, three of them were from Cincinnati—the Liedertafel, the Cincinnati Saengerbund, and the Turner Singing Society. The Newport Saengerbund also participated.[34]

People's Theater at Vine and Thirteenth Streets was the site of the 1856 Saengerfest, which had three hundred participants from nine choirs. Czech conductor and composer Hans Balatka (1825-1899), the leading choral conductor of his time, served as director. Balatka was the founder of the Milwaukee Musical Society and the reputation he gained through his efforts there led to his involvement in the 1856 Saengerfest.[35] Unfortunately, the programs for this festival are lost.[36]

Cincinnati's 1870 Saengerfest was held in a new hall built expressly for the occasion. This was the first time the event had been held in the Queen City since the end of the Civil War, and the older halls would not accommodate all of the 1,800 participants. To alleviate the problem, a large 27,500 square-foot wooden structure was built on a 3.5 acre site in the 1200 block of Elm Street, the present site of Music Hall. Saengerfest Hall was also called Exposition Hall because of the industrial expositions that were held there and in several adjacent structures.

The Music Director of the 1870 festival was Philip Walter, who conducted the three concerts on June 15, 16, and 18.[37]

An article from the *New York Times* on June 16, 1870, describes in colorful detail the fervor with which Cincinnati greeted the Saengerfest. Leading to Saengerfest Hall was a grand procession that paraded through the downtown area. Storefronts were decorated and businesses were closed for the event. The three-mile-long procession took a full hour to pass and an estimated 150,000 people watched, representing almost three-fourths of the city's population. The report continues:

"The houses in almost all parts of the city were more or less decorated, but on the line of

YEAR	CITY	NUMBER OF SOCIETIES	NUMBER OF SINGERS
1849	Cincinnati, OH	5	118
1850	Louisville, KY	7	125
1851	Cincinnati, OH	13	247
1852	Columbus, OH	12	200
1853	Dayton, OH	8	121
1854	Canton, OH	12	146
1855	Cleveland, OH	8	200
1856	Cincinnati, OH	9	300
1857	Detroit, MI	17	144
1858	Pittsburgh, PA	16	200
1859	Cleveland, OH	24	400
1860	Buffalo, NY	25	450
1861-64	N/A	N/A	N/A
1865	Columbus, OH	17	300
1866	Louisville, KY	31	800
1867	Indianapolis, IN	34	1000
1868	Chicago, IL	58	1200
1870	Cincinnati, OH	61	1800
1872	St. Louis, MO	52	1400
1874	Cleveland, OH	56	1600
1877	Louisville, KY	32	1000
1889	Cincinnati, OH	39	1100
1881	Chicago, IL	46	1400
1883	Buffalo, NY	72	2100
1886	Milwaukee, WI	85	2482

Table 2: Saengerfests of the Nord-Amerikanischer Saengerbund, 1849-2013[33]

march an extensive display has been made. An immense arch has been thrown over Fourth-street, near Pike's Opera Hall, and another over Vine-street, opposite Saenger[fest] Hall. Young girls, dressed in white, were placed on each arch, with a banner and wreath of flowers, and presented bouquets to the members of the societies as they passed. Everywhere in the German part of the city the decorations were such as have never been seen here, and other parts of the city were scarcely behind in this respect. Many of the societies have brought bands, embracing some of the most distinguished in the West.... The address of welcome was made by Gov. [Rutherford B.] Hayes."[38]

Philip Walter conducted a 75-piece orchestra for the first and third of these performances, but the number was augmented to 156 for the second concert.

1888	St. Louis, MO	80	2298
1890	New Orleans, LA	64	1700
1893	Cleveland, OH	85	2200
1896	Pittsburgh, PA	80	2300
1899	Cincinnati, OH	64	2757
1901	Buffalo, NY	85	2600
1903	St. Louis, MO	99	3037
1908	Indianapolis, IN	120	2261
1911	Milwaukee, WI	105	3649
1914	Louisville, KY	121	3007
1924	Chicago, IL	84	3870
1927	Cleveland, OH	126	3000
1930	Detroit, MI	115	4242
1934	St. Louis, MO	100	2500
1938	Chicago, IL	181	5882
1949	Chicago, IL	103	3190
1952	Cincinnati, OH	69	2146
1955	Detroit, MI	102	2000
1958	New Orleans, LA	28	700
1961	Milwaukee, WI	65	2200
1964	St. Louis, MO	106	2300
1967	Pittsburgh, PA	66	1800
1970	Columbus, OH	68	2100
1973	Milwaukee, WI	72	2400
1977	Chicago, IL	69	1800
1980	Detroit, MI	59	1400
1983	Columbus, OH	69	2300
1986	Cleveland, OH	60	1600
1989	Louisville, KY	61	1725
1992	Omaha, NE	70	1475
1995	Canton, OH	62	1800
1998	Columbus, OH	64	1875
2001	Chicago, IL	60	1500
2004	Peoria, IL	63	1700
2007	Evansville, IN	69	1500
2010	San Antonio, TX		
2013	Milwaukee, WI		

Table 2 Continued: Saengerfests of the Nord-Amerikanischer Saengerbund, 1849-2013[33]

Programming was of the potpourri variety, as the concerts included orchestral works, concertos, solo arias, and the usual German choral fare. C. L. Fischer, the Royal Prussian Bandmaster of Hanover, composed an original work for male chorus entitled *Heimath* (Homeland). Mrs. Edmund [Emma] Dexter, the British-born wife of a Cincinnati whiskey baron, was soloist on the second concert and performed two works, an unspecified aria from Mozart's *The Marriage of Figaro* and the "Shadow Dance" from Meyerbeer's *Dinorah*. She had studied in London with the illustrious singing teachers Manuel Garcia, who had taught Jenny Lind, and Francesco Schira. If a review of a performance with the Harvard Symphony Orchestra in 1877 is any indication, Mrs. Dexter was an able musician:

"That she could sing it all correctly and

Music Hall appears larger than life in this engraving from 1879. Visitors today will notice that the streetcar tracks remain along Elm Street. However, the angel atop the central spire was never added.

Shown here in winter, Music Hall rises above modern-day Over-the-Rhine as a noble reminder of the neighborhood's former glory. The entire neighborhood is currently undergoing a dramatic renaissance.

in perfect tune, in the true tempi and with just conception and expression, as she did, was enough to prove an artist. Her voice is a large and powerful soprano, mezzo in quality, but of high range, evenly developed, a little thick in the middle tones, but very clear and beautiful in some of the highest; her method sound; phrasing and execution of the best. It was good honest, large, artistic singing."[39]

By the time of the Cleveland Saengerfest in 1874, major musical problems plagued the festivals. Although the number of participants had increased in recent years, the quality of the festival chorus had decreased. The organizers believed that many of the singers traveling to the festivals "cared less for industrious rehearsing than they did for industrious refreshing."[40] The Saengerbund decided that action was needed

and agreed to a new set of rules to help alleviate the problem. No society with fewer than twelve members would be admitted to future Saengerfests. All participating societies would be visited by the conductor's assistant in their home cities to determine whether the individual singers knew the music well enough to take part in the festival. It was also in Cleveland that the Nord-Amerikanischer Saengerbund voted to allow mixed choruses. Although these measures increased the quality and scope of the events, many societies were offended and participation decreased from 1,600 singers at the 1874 Cleveland Saengerfest to just 1,000 at the next festival in Louisville in 1877.[41]

In 1879 the Nord-Amerikanischer Saengerbund held its twenty-first Saengerfest in Cincinnati's newly constructed Music Hall,

Pictures from left to right: Otto Singer was the leader of the Cincinnati Maennerchor and the Cincinnati Musik Verein. He was also chorus master of the May Festival in 1875, 1878, and 1880. People's Theatre on the corner of Vine and Thirteenth Streets was the site of the 1856 Saengerfest. The lobby area now houses the Venice On Vine restaurant. Pike's Opera House was the venue of choice for opera productions in Cincinnati. Emma Heckle was a noted soprano who based her career in Cincinnati.

Singing Schools, Social

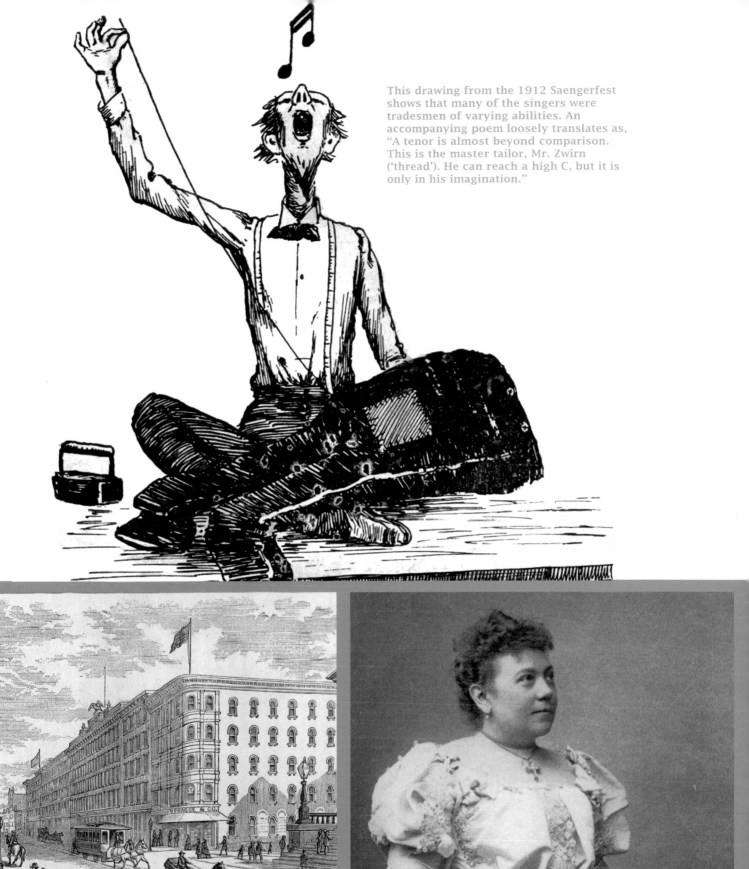

This drawing from the 1912 Saengerfest shows that many of the singers were tradesmen of varying abilities. An accompanying poem loosely translates as, "A tenor is almost beyond comparison. This is the master tailor, Mr. Zwirn ('thread'). He can reach a high C, but it is only in his imagination."

Music Hall as it appeared looking across Washington Park about 1890. The College of Music buildings are visible next to the hall in the space now occupied by a parking lot.

All discussions of music in Cincinnati eventually turn to the city's temple of music, Music Hall. When the May Festivals of 1873 and 1875 were interrupted by rain and hail resonating from the tin roof of Saengerfest Hall,[1] the septuagenarian Cincinnati railroad magnate Reuben Springer proposed that a new hall be built before the third May Festival. He gave $125,000 to the project, but two conditions applied: the city had to provide the lot and offer reasonable rent with no taxation, and the citizens of Cincinnati had to match the money he offered. Although Springer claimed that the new hall would be used for music and industrial expositions, business leaders were reluctant to lend their support. To that end, Springer offered and additional $50,000, if $100,000 more could be raised from the public. This money was earmarked for two exposition buildings to be constructed on either side of the new Music Hall. In the end, 384 people contributed and exceeded the challenge grant. Of the total, $3,000 came from small change contributed by local schoolchildren.[2]

The Cincinnati Music Hall Association, an organization formed to oversee the project, hired the architectural firm of Hannaford and Procter to design the new facility. Their plan was approved and construction began on May 1, 1877, just a year before the third May Festival was to begin. The design was ambitious. Music Hall would be 150 feet tall at its central gable. Of its 372 feet of frontage, 178 feet was devoted to the main hall, while nearly 90 feet would be occupied by each of the two exposition buildings. The building would be 293 feet deep from Elm Street to the Miami and Erie Canal that flowed behind the hall. Above the elaborate lobby would be a small hall that eventually would be named for Julius Dexter, the chairman of the building committee. The main hall, which would be named to honor Reuben Springer, would be 192 feet long and 112 feet wide, and the stage would cover an impressive 6,272 square feet. A balcony at the back and sides of Springer Hall would allow additional seating.[3] No gallery was included in the original design. Cincinnati's Music Hall was dedicated on May 14 at the first concert of the 1878 May Festival. The exposition buildings would not be completed until the following year.

Before the hall could be built, an important matter had to be solved. The area bordered north and south by Twelfth and Fourteenth Streets and east and west by the canal and Race Street had been the site of several cemeteries. Just west of the canal was the Community Hospital and Insane Asylum, and the Pest House sat just south on the same lot. When inmates or patients expired, they were interred in Potter's Field, the present site of Music Hall. Over two hundred wagon loads of bones were moved to Spring Grove Cemetery and reburied in a mass grave. Stories of hauntings in the hall survive to this day.

After the successful 1878 May Festival, the hall and exposition buildings found several additional uses. The 1880 convention of the Democratic Party was held in Music Hall. Delegates chose General Winfield Scott Hancock as their presidential candidate, but he would narrowly lose the election to Ohioan James A. Garfield. Almost annually, industrial expositions were housed in the twin exposition buildings. From 1880 until 1882 the Cincinnati Tennis Club played on a court in the south hall. In 1883 electric lighting was introduced to Cincinnati at the Eleventh Industrial Exposition.[4]

Of course, Music Hall has undergone many changes in its more than 130 years. A major renovation took place in 1896 in preparation for the one-year-old Cincinnati Symphony Orchestra's move to the facility from Pike's Opera House. Construction was extensive, involving the addition of a new stage, proscenium arch, gallery seating, electric lights, steam heat, and permanent seating. The second balcony was also built at this time. In 1905 Arthur Thomas painted the circular Allegory of the Arts on the ceiling of Springer Auditorium. In 1927 the second story of the south exposition building was converted to a new ballroom called the Topper Club. Two years later it would be decorated with an Egyptian motif, and a full-size replica of the Sphinx would be placed in front of the building. Maintenance of Music Hall was taken over by the city of Cincinnati in 1941. During that decade, the north exposition building was converted to a six thousand seat sports complex that was used for boxing, wrestling, and University of Cincinnati basketball games.[5]

The last major renovation took place between 1968 and 1975, through the generosity of Cincinnati philanthropists J. Ralph and Patricia Corbett. Air conditioning was added (resulting in the bricked windows), along with escalators, chandeliers, a pit elevator, an expanded scene shop, an audio system, stage rigging, and a new theater curtain. The backstage area was revamped to include numerous dressing rooms and a new green room. In 1972 Dexter Hall was renamed Corbett Tower. In 1998 the shell of the old Topper Club was reborn as Music Hall Ballroom. Since 1969 the Cincinnati Symphony and Cincinnati Opera offices have been located in Music Hall, first in the south exposition building. In 2002, the Corbett Foundation provided funding to convert the north exposition building into the Corbett Opera Center, which houses the offices of the Cincinnati Opera along with modern rehearsal spaces.[6] Renovations aimed at modernizing the hall and reducing seating capacity are set to begin in 2012.

Currently, Music Hall is the venue for Cincinnati's premiere musical organizations. The Cincinnati Symphony Orchestra performed there from 1896 until 1911 and from 1936 to the present after spending some years at Emery Auditorium. The Cincinnati Opera performances came to Music Hall in 1972 after fifty-two years at an open-air pavilion at the Cincinnati Zoo. Cincinnati's May Festival has taken place in Springer Auditorium since 1878.

This is a rare photo of Music Hall in its original configuration in 1888. Note the folding chairs and ceremonial decorations, most likely for the Centennial Exposition of the Ohio Valley held in the hall that year. On May 14, 1878, Music Hall held its inaugural opening night for the May Festival. This somewhat exaggerated drawing shows an audience of over 7,000, almost double the 4,500 seats available that evening. J. Ralph and Patricia Corbett were among Cincinnati's most benevolent philanthropists. Among their most important contributions were the many improvements they made to Music Hall, including air conditioning, chandeliers, stage equipment, and office space for the Cincinnati Opera.

1. This should not be confused with the Jubilee Saengerfest Hall, which was built in 1899.
2. Robert C. Vitz, *The Queen and the Arts: Cultural Life in Nineteenth-Century Cincinnati* (Kent, Ohio, and London, England: Kent State University Press 1989), 96-98.
3. "The Music Hall," *Cincinnati Daily Gazette*, May 11, 1878, 1.
4. Charles H. Parsons, *A Celebration of Cincinnati Opera* (Cincinnati: privately printed, 2007), 280.
5. Ibid., 281.
6. Ibid., 281-283.

Rhine to an uptown location across the street from the Cincinnati Zoological Gardens on what is now a parking lot.

Ground was broken on February 20, 1899, just four months before the festival, and the hall was not completed by opening day, which forced the Jubilee Saengerfest to open one day late.[51] As the delay was not publicized, fifteen thousand people gathered outside awaiting entry to a hall whose stage and flooring had not been completed. Early on the morning of opening day, "Supervising Architect Ward Baldwin ... [realized] that he could not keep his promise to have the hall ready to-night and he broke down under the strain. He is pronounced to be in a very serious condition from nervous prostration."[52] Police set up barricades to restrain the disgruntled audience from going inside, but many defeated the barriers. Even orchestra members showed up ready to play. According to the *New York Times*, "[w]hile the crowd was in the building, William Bateman, a workingman, was struck by falling timber and seriously hurt."[53]

The design of Jubilee Saengerfest Hall was unique for its day. It sat diagonally on the rectangular lot to allow triangular spaces for people to gather outside the hall. Seating was on three levels: parquet seats numbered 2,766, with a dress circle accommodating 3,524 and the balcony seating 3,848, for a total capacity of 10,128.[54] A *New York Times* review of the opening concert included the following description.

"The vast interior of the hall can be described as a many times magnified eggshell – the similarity is in shape only, as the vast beams and springing arches and the wilderness of geometric braces suggest a strength altogether different from an eggshell structure. The effect of such a great height and such rounded expanse is to bring the audience and the occupants of the stage into easy companionship. Under the remarkable circumstances of the finishing work on the hall, there was but little opportunity for elaborate decoration, but the interior was brilliantly illuminated with arc lights."[55]

Despite the appearance of the hall,

The architect who sketched the plans for Jubilee Saengerfest Hall saw it as a white Art Nouveau edifice, perhaps inspired by the 1893 Chicago World's Fair and its "White City." The result was a shoddy ten thousand-seat structure fraught with structural problems.

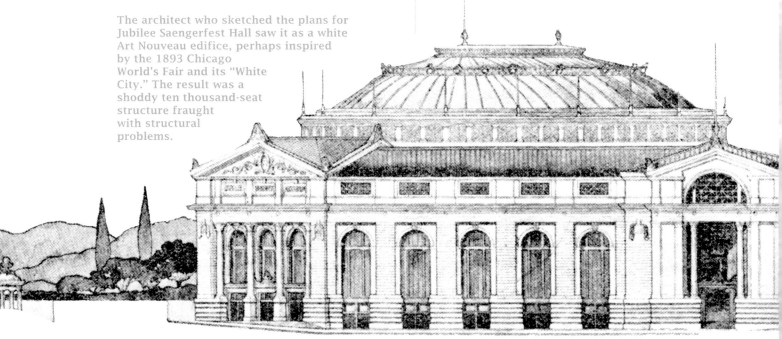

the review mentions that a board fell during the performance, causing a woman to scream.

Because of the delay in opening, visitors were treated to two processions. The usual grand parade took place on the scheduled opening day, June 28, 1899, but an impromptu "burlesque [caricature] on street parades" occurred on the following day. Visiting societies dressed according to themes, which resulted in marching depictions of Sousa's band, Theodore Roosevelt's Rough Riders, and the beery cheerfulness of Gambrinus and his followers.[56]

Those who sat in the hall's ten thousand seats and hundreds of others, who crowded into every possible foot of standing room for the five festival concerts, witnessed a spectacle they would never forget. Each concert began with an overture, Beethoven's *Consecration of the House*, Saint-Saëns's *Phaëton*, and Mozart's *Don Giovanni* among them. Although the soloists were not as famous as those in the 1879 Cincinnati Saengerfest, they were well received and offered a wide range of repertoire. Sara Anderson performed arias by Delibes, Liszt, and Wagner. Soprano Charlotta Maconda performed the Mad Scene from Donizetti's *Lucia di Lammermoor*. Another soprano, Corinne Moore-Lawson, sang Schubert's "The Shepherd on the Rock" and a few art songs. While the repertoire of the soloists was not strictly German, the contributions of the choruses on these concerts reflected mostly the German Maennerchor tradition.[57]

After the 1899 festival, the Nord-Amerikanischer Saengerbund continued

its festivals, which grew in participation, but increasing anti-German sentiment led to breaks in the festivities during both World Wars, and no Saengerfests were held between 1914-24 and 1939-1949. The peak of participation was at the 1938 Chicago festival, which had nearly six thousand participants. Cincinnati hosted the 1952 Saengerfest, but only two thousand singers attended. The Nord-Amerikanischer Saengerbund is still in operation and its next Saengerfest is scheduled for 2013 in Milwaukee. Locally, the Cincinnati Catholic Kolping Society has carried on the tradition since the formation of its Saengerchor in 1989 by Carolann and Jim Slouffman. The organization is a branch of the Kolping Society founded in the 1860s by Adolf Kolping in Cologne, Germany. As members of the Nord-Amerikanischer Saengerbund, they continue to carry the banner.

CINCINNATI MAY FESTIVAL

incinnati's famous May Festival, first given in 1873, is a unique mixture of English and German choral traditions. The founders were representatives of both backgrounds. While the artistic forces were almost entirely German, the administrative team that planned the event was mostly of English descent. Cincinnati's successful 1870 Saengerfest was certainly a hometown model for the May Festival, but the tone of the event came from the spectacularly large but well-mannered display of the large massed-choir traditions of English festivals in Leeds and elsewhere. The festive social component of the German festivals, complete with food and drink, has never been a regular part of the May Festival. At the time of this writing, the festival is 138 years old and has been a continuing event since its inception in 1873. Until 1967 the May Festival was held every two years with only a few exceptions, but since then it has been given every year. Over the years, many people have held the positions of Music Director and Chorus Master, as may be seen in Tables 3a and 3b. As it is impossible to consider every one of the ninety-two festivals, as of 2012, this section will consider the origins of the May Festival and landmark events at selected festivals.

The story of the May Festival actually begins ten years before the first official event. In October of 1863, a circular was sent to the "Musical Public of Cincinnati" to extend "a cordial invitation to singers, both ladies and gentlemen, who will take an interest in building up a large Choral Society, such as the old societies of Boston and New York, to join."[59] In January of 1864 this Musical Union renamed itself the Harmonic Society. The leader was Carl Barus, who had recently been the leader of Cincinnati Maennerchor. The 116 singers gave

a performance of Mendelssohn's *St. Paul* sometime in 1864. This mixed chorus approach to presenting oratorio with members drawn from a broad spectrum of Cincinnati's singers, regardless of the nationality or society to which they pledged allegiance, must be regarded as an important precedent of the May Festival.

The traditional story of the founding of the Cincinnati May Festival in 1873 is one that has taken on the proportions of a folk tale and conflicts greatly with the facts told by documents of the time. Cincinnati history usually holds that, on one undated Sunday evening in 1872, Maria (pronounced with a long "I") Longworth Nichols, the twenty-three-year-old granddaughter of Nicholas Longworth—one of the wealthiest Cincinnatians and owner of Eden Park, "most of the West End," and "half of Walnut Hills"—invited the famous conductor Theodore Thomas to her home on Grandin Road to discuss an idea that she had been formulating for some time.[60] She realized that, since Thomas was in

MUSIC DIRECTOR	
1873–1904	Theodore Thomas
1906–1912	Frank Van der Stucken
1914–1916	Ernst Kunwald
1918–1920	Eugene Ysaÿe
1923–1927	Frank Van der Stucken
1929	Frederick Stock
1931–1946	Eugene Goossens
1948–1950	Fritz Busch
1952	Thor Johnson, Jean Morel, Fritz Stiedry (guest conductors)
1954–1960	Josef Krips
1963, 1967–1970	Max Rudolf
1965	Stanislaw Skrowaczewski, Robert Shaw (guest conductors)
1971–1972	Julius Rudel
1973	Leonard Bernstein (honorary)
1974–1978	James Levine
1979–present	James Conlon

Table 3a: May Festival Music Directors

town giving a concert, the time was right to propose to him that he conduct what is today the oldest continuing choral music festival in the Western Hemisphere. According to Sheblessy's account of the meeting, the participants were Maria; her husband, Colonel George Ward Nichols, who had been an aide-de-camp to Civil War Generals Fremont and Sherman; Heinrich Rattermann, a leading figure in the Saengerfests of the past decade; Henry Krehbiel, music critic of the *Cincinnati Gazette*; and Thomas.[61] Sheblessy wrongly implies that the meeting ended with the establishment of the Cincinnati Musical Festival Association and the doling out of offices within its structure.

The program notes of the 1988 May Festival honoring the Saengerfests, in a more realistic, less grandiose version, attribute Maria Longworth Nichols' eagerness to have a festival in Cincinnati to an 1871 trip to England, where she witnessed one of the large English festivals. At home, Mr. Nichols was a member of the Harmonic Society, so the couple was involved in choral music of the English variety. Thomas, during their meeting in 1872, agreed to be conductor of the Festival if fifty thousand dollars could be raised for a guarantee fund and a committee could be formed to take care of the business aspects of the event.[62] Thomas wrote:

"On my ... visit in 1871 [*sic*–it was 1872] a young married lady [Maria Longworth Nichols], member of one of the leading families, laid before me a plan for a large Musical Festival. She proposed that I should be the conductor of it, saying that if I would be responsible for the artistic side, she would find the men who would take charge of the business details. I soon found out that this lady was not only very talented in many ways, but that her taste was not amateurish in anything, and I readily consented to undertake the work she wished me to do. Some of the programs were sketched at her home."[63]

The role of Mrs. Nichols in the planning of the Festival during initial stages is not documented. Nowhere in the extant papers of the Cincinnati Musical Festival Association

CHORUS MASTER	
1873, 1882	Carl Barus
1875, 1878, 1880	Otto Singer
1882, 1886	Arthur Mees
1884, 1898-1904	Edwin Glover
1888, 1890, 1918	Louis Ehrgott
1892-1896	W.L. Blumenschein
1908-1944	Alfred Hartzel
1946-1948	Sherwood Kains
1950-1960	Willis Beckett
1963-1969	Robert Knauf
1970-1973, 1975	Elmer Thomas
1974	Earl Rivers (acting)
1976-1978	Thomas Peck
1979-1988	John Leman
1989	John H. Williams
1990	Robert Porco

Table 3b: May Festival Chorus Masters[58]

is she given even cursory mention. It seems that her role was simply that of a facilitator who was from a prominent family that had sold the 209 acres of Eden Park to the city just seven years earlier for the huge sum of $800,000, and thus her involvement in any capacity would have commanded the attention of other wealthy Cincinnatians.[64] However, that she would be mentioned at all by Thomas and others attests to her having great influence in the planning of the Festival. Her biographer, Sr. Rose Angela Boehle, mentions that Maria and Col. Nichols started the guarantee fund of the 1873 Festival with a five-thousand-dollar contribution. After this, "George stayed with the musical development of the Queen City while his wife devoted her time and energy to art."[65] At the beginning of the next decade she founded Rookwood Pottery. Thus it seems

that influence and money may have been her only contributions to the May Festival beyond her initial imaginative vision. Of course, the absence of her name from the official records might also reflect the limited role that women were permitted to have in such undertakings in the late nineteenth century. Maria's idea was prophetic, both artistically and musically, but the degree to which all elements came together to form a lasting and significant festival in a city on the eastern edge of the western frontier remains astounding to this day.

The day-to-day work of planning the festival began on Friday, September 27, 1872, at 10:00 a.m. in the law offices of Storer, Goodman, and Storer at 6 West Third Street in downtown Cincinnati, where the Cincinnati Musical Festival Association's Executive Committee was formed. George Ward Nichols was appointed

Pictures from left to right: The founders of the May Festival included soon-to-be Rookwood Pottery founder Maria Longworth Nichols, dry goods merchant George W. Jones, attorney Bellamy Storer, Jr., music publisher and merchant John Church, founder of the famous department store John Shillito, and amateur singer and Civil War veteran Col. George Ward Nichols.

President, with Carl A. G. Adae, a German-born banker and Consul at Frankfurt-am-Main for the states of Ohio and Indiana, as Vice President, dry goods merchant John Shillito as treasurer, Cincinnati music publisher and merchant John Church as Chairman of the Printing Committee, and attorney Bellamy Storer, Jr., as Secretary. George W. Jones, a dry goods merchant and president of the Miami Valley Insurance Company, joined the Executive Committee four days later. A month later, lumber yard owner Daniel Buell Pierson became the final member. Over the following eight months, these men made all of the business decisions leading to the May Festival of 1873.[66]

After the preliminaries, the next order of business was to decide on artistic matters. Among the first actions of the Executive Committee was the hiring of Theodore Thomas as musical director and Carl Barus as director of the chorus. Thomas's touring orchestra would play, as they would continue to do at every festival until 1904. Arthur Mees, a Cincinnati music teacher, was named rehearsal accompanist and, later, festival organist. A circular describing the expectations of chorus members was printed in English and German and distributed to 121 music dealers, 60 post offices, and 144 singing societies. It was also distributed to 1,120 newspapers throughout Ohio, Indiana, Kentucky, and "the leading papers of the West."[67] A committee of the Cincinnati Chorus, including presidents of the Harmonic, Orpheus, Germania, and St. Cecilia Societies, and the Cincinnati, Druiden, and Harugari Maennerchore, was named to find members for the festival chorus and establish an expectation of high artistic standards. Rehearsals were set to begin in January.[68]

Sometime in November, the Executive Committee decided to address the naming of soloists. Thomas reserved the right to veto any artistic decision, so there is a large amount of correspondence on this issue. Thomas

Columbia Street Theatre
Southwest corner of Columbia (now Second), between Main and Sycamore
Capacity: 600-800
Opened: March 8, 1820
Closed: April 4, 1834, burned

People's Theatre
Northwest corner of Fourth and Walnut
Capacity: N/A
Opened: March 26, 1845
Closed: January 8, 1848, burned during a heavy snowstorm

Pike's Opera House
South side of Fourth, between Vine and Walnut
Capacity: 1859-1866, 3,000; 1868-1903, 2,000
Opened: March 1859, Reopened February 12, 1868
Closed: March 22, 1866, burned February 25, 1903, burned

Grand Opera House
Corner of Longworth and Vine (presently 200 block of Vine)
Capacity: 2,400
Opened: September 7, 1874, Reopened September 15, 1902 as New Grand Opera House
Closed: January 22, 1901, burned. 1940, closed

National Theatre
East side of Sycamore, between Third and Fourth
Capacity: 2,500
Opened: July 3, 1837
Closed: After 1880 it was used as a tobacco warehouse. Razed in 1940.

Robinson's Opera House
Northest corner of Plum and Ninth
Capacity: 1,800
Opened: December 20, 1872
Closed: razed in 1936.

Saengerfest Hall
Southwest corner of Fourteenth and Elm
Capacity: ca. 5,000, but 7,000 if aisles were filled
Opened: 1870
Closed: 1875, razed to build Music Hall

Smith & Nixon's Hall
24 W. Fourth Street, between Main and Walnut
Capacity: N/A
Opened: 1853
Closed: ca. 1890

Zoo
Vine and Erkenbrecher
Capacity: Variable
Opened: September 18, 1875.

Melodeon Hall
Northwest corner of Fourth and Walnut
Capacity: N/A
Opened: 1846
Closed: 1867, burned

Wood's Theatre
Southeast corner of Sixth and Vine
Capacity: 1,240, after 1869, 1720
Opened: November 1, 1856
Closed: June 1878, razed for business block

Highland House
Head of Mt. Adams Incline
Capacity: 6,000-8,000
Opened: About 1875
Closed: razed about 1895.

Shellbark Theatre
South Side of Columbia (now Second), between Main and Sycamore
Capacity: N/A
Opened: March 15, 1815
Closed: Late 1819, when it was razed to build Columbia Street Theatre

Under various ownership:
Atheneum Theatre, American Theatre, Olympic Theatre, New Lyceum Theatre, People's Theatre
Southeast corner of Sixth and Vine
Capacity: N/A
Opened: April 26, 1847
Closed: June 1856, burned

Mozart Hall
Corner of Longworth and Vine
Capacity: 3,000
Opened: 1863
Closed: 1874, converted to Grand Opera House

Coliseum Opera House
Vine, between Twelfth and Thirteenth
Capacity: 2,000-2,500, plus standing room
Opened: December 23, 1876
Closed: May 1883, razed for Heuck's New Opera House

Third Street Theatre
South side of Third, between Broadway and Sycamore, extending to Lower Market Street
Capacity: 1,300
Opened: July 4, 1832
Closed: October 21, 1836, burned

1815 · 1820 · 1832 · 1837 · 1845 · 1846 · 1847 · 1856 · 1859 · 1863 · 1872 · 1874 · 1875 · 1876

Heuck's Opera House

Northwest corner Vine and Thirteenth
Capacity: 1,900
Opened: June 18, 1877;
November 17, 1883,
name changed to
People's Theatre
Closed: 1921

Harris's Theatre

Vine, near Sixth. Later, in Robinson's Opera House
Capacity: 2,300
Opened: 1883
Closed: 1893

Walnut Street Theatre

East side of Walnut, between Sixth and Seventh
Capacity: 1,600
Opened: September 26, 1892
Closed: 1916

Havlin's Theatre

West side of Central Avenue, between Fourth and Fifth
Capacity: 2,300
Opened: 1883
Closed: 1895

Emery Auditorium

Northeast corner of Walnut and East Central Parkway
Capacity: 2,200
Opened: 1911
Closed: 1988
Reopened 2011.

Jubilee Saengerfest Hall

Southwest corner of Erkenbrecher and Vine, across from the Cincinnati Zoo
Capacity: 10,128
Opened: June 29, 1899
Closed: Razed 1901

Music Hall

Southwest corner of Fourteenth and Elm
Capacity: 1878-1895,
4,500; 1896-1969, 4,200;
1969-2013, 2,416;
proposed renovation in
2012, 1,900
Opened: 1878

Odeon

Elm and Grant, adjacent to Music Hall
Capacity: 1,200
Opened: October 1884
Closed: September 5, 1902, burned

Chester Park

North side of Spring Grove Avenue at Platt Avenue
Capacity: N/A
Opened: 1878
Closed: 1932

Heuck's New Opera House

Northwest corner of Vine and Thirteenth
Capacity: N/A
Opened: 1883
Closed: 1921

For a city to have as much musical activity as Cincinnati, it is necessary that it be graced with many stages. Some choruses have established their homes in Cincinnati's many churches, but others required theaters and concert halls in which to perform. Many of these halls were short-lived, largely because the gas lights that illuminated nineteenth-century theaters would ignite curtains and draperies used to decorate the interior.

The table on the left is a list of the most prominent theaters and halls used for opera and concerts from 1815 until 2012. Facilities built specifically for vaudeville, burlesque, or movies are not included, although some on the list were later converted for that purpose. The timeline that shows the relative lifespan of each of the buildings.

	1800	1825	1850	1875	1900	1925	1950	1975	2000
Shellbark Theatre									
Columbia Street Theatre									
Third Street Theatre									
National Theatre									
People's Theatre									
Melodeon Hall									
Athenaeum, American, Olympic, New Lyceum, People's Theatre									
Smith & Nixon's Hall									
Wood's Theatre									
Pike's Opera House									
Mozart Hall									
Saengerfest Hall									
Robinson's Opera House									
Grand Opera House									
Highland House									
Chester Park									
Zoo									
Coliseum Opera House									
Heuck's Opera House/People's Theatre									
Music Hall									
Heuck's New Opera House									
Odeon									
Havlin's Theatre									
Harris's Theatre									
Walnut Street Theatre									
Julbilee Saengerfest Hall									
Emery Auditorium									

upward and forward. Back of the orchestra, and reared high above it is the mammoth organ, neatly draped."[76]

Performances included repertoire that was overwhelmingly German. Handel, Bach, Beethoven, Haydn, and Mozart comprised the first two concerts. Of the sixty works on the seven concerts, only five were by composers not born in a German-speaking country. The matinee concerts consisted largely of arias, art songs, and light orchestral works, including isolated movements of symphonies, Strauss waltzes, and overtures. Thomas's evening concerts were more formal and consisted of major vocal and choral works, including Handel's *Dettingen Te Deum*, scenes from Gluck's *Orfeo ed Euridice*, and Beethoven's Ninth Symphony, along with purely symphonic works and concert arias.

Critical reception was overwhelmingly favorable. Of Annie Louis Cary's rendition of the Gluck excerpts, the *Cincinnati Gazette* remarked:

"She carried all hearts by storm in her singing of this part. Her pronunciation, so distinct, without effort or mouthing, enabled the audience to appreciate the truth of her expression. The 'recitatives,' so trying to the 'barrel organ' order of vocalists, were as musical as the 'arias'... and there was nowhere the vulgar attempt at ornamentation of which an inferior singer would have been guilty."[77]

Local soprano Emma Dexter was greeted with adulation, as related by the *Cincinnati Commercial*:

"In this aria Mrs. Dexter more than met the highest anticipations of her friends, and won the admiration of the entire audience by the flexibility, purity and sympathetic timbre of her voice. So beautiful was one of her veiled high trills that applause burst forth inopportunely in the very middle of a bar. Her applause, like Miss Cary's, had the unusual ingredient of cheers. The demand for a repetition was imperative, and, of course, Mrs. Dexter acceded to it gracefully."[78]

However, the most abundant praise of the week was for the Thursday night performance of Beethoven's Ninth Symphony. *Dwight's Journal of Music*, a Boston paper consisting of reviews written in Boston from telegraphed accounts of reporters, described the scene after the conclusion of the Ninth:

"The last notes had scarcely died away before the entire eight thousand people within the building were on their feet. Madness seemed to rule the hour. Amid a whirlwind of cheers, stamping, laughing, and we might almost say without exaggeration, crying, calls were heard of 'Thomas! Thomas!' 'The Chorus! The Chorus!' 'Cary! Cary!' 'Singer! Singer!'[79], and so on until the leader had bowed his acknowledgments again and again. Even then the people departed reluctantly, and not before a score of pretty girls from the chorus had forced their way into the lady soloist's dressing room and raped kisses from the overjoyed prima donna contralto."[80]

In the five days from May 6-10, 1873, Cincinnati's reputation as a city of Saengerfests grew to include world-class performances of canonic works for orchestra and chorus. When news of the upcoming Chicago Festival was announced during the Cincinnati May Festival of 1873, the *Chicago Tribune*, as quoted in *Church's Musical Visitor* (published by Executive Committee member John Church, Jr.), expressed concern over the prospects of assembling a chorus and put the question of the worth of the first Cincinnati May Festival to rest once and for all:

"It is morally certain that we have not now the material for any chorus at all. There is not a society of mixed voices in Chicago. It might be possible to organize a small chorus, by dint of hard labor, which, in the course of time, would be able to produce such music as was sung in Cincinnati, but to establish a large and competent chorus seems well nigh impossible. Chicago, like New York, is a cosmopolitan city, with a changeable population, and spread over a great area of territory. It is only an old and stationary population of leisure and wealth which can produce such a chorus. New York could not do it, and so the Boston Handel and Haydn Society was imported for the occasion of the festival in that city. Cincinnati had the material at home, and its singers submitted to a drill and discipline which were rightly severe, and at the close of the festival were as enthusiastic as when they commenced. The result of that festival to-day is, that Cincinnati is the first musical city of the West."[81]

A second May Festival took place at Saengerfest Hall in 1875, and presented the American premieres of Bach's *Magnificat* and Brahms's *Triumphlied*. During this festival, Cincinnati's usual springtime thunderstorms pelted the leaky tin roof of the hall with rain and hail, as they had done to a lesser degree in 1873. The cavernous hall acted as a resonating chamber and Thomas had to stop the concerts on more than one occasion to let the storms

pass. Two other problems with the hall were mentioned in the press reports of the first festival, which no doubt persisted in 1875. The reporter from the *Gazette* mentioned that the temperature in the hall was too warm. The situation was "promptly remedied by a member of the Executive Committee who crashed out the glass from every window whose frame was wedged too tight in its place to be readily moved."[82] Another problem arose as the audience, estimated at four thousand with two thousand more in the streets, seems to have grown somewhat frustrated by the crowded conditions in the hall and complained that allowing one thousand people to stand in the aisles "sorely disappoints ticket-holders who selected their seats on the aisles with especial purpose."[83] These breaches of decorum no doubt troubled Thomas, but he was not alone. Kentucky-born railroad entrepreneur Reuben Springer was so annoyed by the situation that he made the initial $125,000 donation to create a matching fund to enable the construction of Music Hall, completed in 1878. The Third May Festival, originally scheduled for 1877 but postponed until the new hall could be finished, cemented the festival as a recurring event deserving of notice on a national level.

After the death of Theodore Thomas in 1905, the 1906 May Festival featured British composer Sir Edward Elgar conducting the American premiere of his oratorio *The Dream of Gerontius* at the final concert. Although Texas-born Frank Van der Stucken, the well-liked

Music Director of the Cincinnati Symphony Orchestra since its formation in 1895, had taken over as director of the May Festival, Thomas's loss was deeply felt. Elgar was the most prominent British composer and much of his music was popular in the U.S. He conducted the second, fifth, and sixth concerts of the festival, and spent the preceding two weeks rehearsing his music with the performers. In a tradition that had begun during the 1873 May Festival, the 1906 affair made use of a chorus of school children. Frank Van der Stucken's large choral work *Pax Triumphans* included a children's chorus of over 1,000. The festival was dedicated to the memory of Thomas.[84]

The 1906 festival was front-page news in the *Cincinnati Commercial* and opening night articles appeared on three pages of the May 2 issue. "Handsome Gowns Worn by Society Folk at Opening" informed readers, among its descriptions of the evening wear displayed by nearly one hundred women from all levels of society, that "Mrs. Elwood Cree was in green crepe de chine." Of course, the heart of the account was the coverage of the musical portion of the concerts. German soprano Johanna Gadski, who had triumphed at the Bayreuth Festival in 1899, performed Brünnhilde's "Immolation Scene" from Wagner's *Götterdämmerung* and the soprano solo in Brahms's *Ein deutsches Requiem*. Of Gadski's Wagner, the *Commercial* commented: "We all know her to be a great artist–one of the greatest–but her work in this magnificent number was certainly unusual even for her."[85]

Even without Thomas, the new era began

Pictures from left to right: Reuben Springer was the father of Music Hall, having provided half of the funds for its construction through a challenge grant. Frank Van der Stucken, founding conductor of the Cincinnati Symphony Orchestra, became music director of the May Festival upon the death of Theodore Thomas. The only known picture of the inside of Saengerfest Hall shows the "steep incline" of the chorus and the "solid railing" in front of the orchestra, as mentioned in a newspaper review of the first May Festival. The "mammoth organ, neatly draped" is visible above. (Courtesy of Craig Doolin)

This rare photograph of Theodore Thomas conducting was taken from the chorus risers onstage at the 1894 May Festival in Music Hall.

with many world-class soloists. An early favorite was the Austrian singer Ernestine Schumann-Heink, who appeared at eight festivals. She was the most famous contralto of her day, partly because of her popular recordings for the new Victrola. Her repertoire was largely German, including Wagner roles at Bayreuth. Schumann-Heink's last appearance at the May Festival was in 1929, when she was sixty-eight years of age.[86] Other prominent soloists of the period were sopranos Alma Gluck, Florence Hinkle, Marcella Sembrich, Jeanette Vreeland, and Lily Pons, tenor Daniel Beddow, baritone Lawrence Tibbett, and basses Ezio Pinza and Herbert Witherspoon.

Over the years, the May Festival has stayed true to its mission of presenting large choral works, many of them rarely heard and several of them American or world premieres. The 1914 festival included the American premiere of Mahler's Symphony No. 3, a sprawling ninety-minute work in six movements that calls for contralto solo and women's and children's choruses. In 1916 Richard Strauss's *Alpine Symphony*, a purely orchestral work but exceedingly grand in scale, had its American premiere. Perhaps the largest work in the repertoire, Mahler's Symphony No. 8, often called *The Symphony of a Thousand*, received a then-rare performance at the 1931 festival with

a chorus of nine hundred, a massive orchestra, and eight soloists. The 1946 May Festival gave the first complete performance of Delius's *A Mass of Life*, and the 1956 festivities included the American premiere of Britten's "Choral Dances" from his opera *Gloriana*, written for the coronation of Queen Elizabeth II in 1953. In 1963 the May Festival commissioned Gian Carlo Menotti to compose an opera, and that work, *The Death of the Bishop of Brindisi*, was premiered on that year's program.[87]

The early 1970s saw controversy and triumph at the May Festival. Music Director Julius Rudel, Director of the New York City Opera, brought the illustrious soprano Beverly Sills and bass Norman Treigle to reprise their roles in the NYCO production of Handel's *Julius Caesar*. The following year, Bernstein's *Mass* thrilled listeners, but caused uproar from local Catholics who opposed its non-liturgical language and found the work to be blasphemous. This controversy created great demand for tickets. Leonard Bernstein was Honorary Music Director for the 1973 centennial celebration of the May Festival, at which he conducted Beethoven's *Missa Solemnis*. Cincinnati-born James Levine became the Music Director in 1974 and served for four seasons, until the present director James Conlon took the helm in 1979.[88]

During times of war and tragedy, the May Festival has traditionally stepped forward to honor heroes and soothe the pain. During World War II, patriotic music held pride of place in 1942 and performers donated their services. All proceeds were given to the Cincinnati War Chest. In 1944 a chorus of Women's Army Corps members from

The last act of Georges Bizet's *Carme* at Cincinnati Opera in 2009. (Courtesy of Philip Groshong)

Cincinnati's musical history began with opera. In 1801 the Thespian Corps, a group consisting of early settlers and the soldiers of Fort Washington in present-day downtown Cincinnati, mounted a performance of *The Poor Soldier* by British author John O'Keefe (1747-1837). This ballad opera consisted of an original overture, adapted Irish airs, and some new vocal numbers. Until about 1860, almost without exception, English ballad opera was the rule in Cincinnati. Most of the works had been premiered in Britain in the late eighteenth century at Covent Garden or Drury Lane; *The Poor Soldier* was first heard at Covent Garden on April 7, 1783. The chorus in Cincinnati consisted of available singers.[1]

As the nineteenth century progressed, the touring companies that visited large cities throughout the United States brought a uniquely American brand of European opera. Even works that were composed to be sung throughout were given spoken dialogue in America. Melodrama, essentially a drama with instrumental underscoring, was usually presented with inserted songs. Theatrical spectacles became quite popular because of the elaborate scenery, stage effects, and theatrical machines.[2] Of course, local productions existed, but these mimicked the touring companies.

Until the founding of the Cincinnati Opera in 1920, most formal operatic offerings in the Queen City were given by touring companies. Italian opera, sung in the original language, was first heard here in 1843, performed by a band of Italian singers on the way to New York from Havana by way of the port of New Orleans and the Mississippi and Ohio Rivers.[3] English opera companies presented original English operas and English translations of European, mainly Italian, operas. German works reached Cincinnati for the first time in 1860 and waned in popularity until regaining some ground in the 1890s. French opera remained a minor attraction after it was first heard in the city in the late 1860s.

Unfortunately, early reviews rarely mention choruses. When they are singled out, it is usually to draw attention to deficiencies. It must be assumed that most of the operas heard in Cincinnati had chorus parts, but there is no guarantee that these parts were actually performed. For example, in November of 1874, Cincinnati's first production of Verdi's *Aïda*, known for its choruses and spectacle, received accolades from the *Cincinnati Enquirer*, but there was no specific mention of the chorus.[4]

Beginning in 1881, the Board of Trustees of the College of Music attempted to gain financial support by sponsoring a series of opera festivals performed by the major touring companies of the day. The choruses contained students, and leading singers of the day performed the major roles. Adelina Patti, Christine Nilsson, and Marcella Sembrich were among those who delighted audiences in largely Italian fare, including *Il Trovatore*, *Don Giovanni*, *Lucia di Lammermoor*, and an Italian translation of *Die Zauberflöte*, but German and French works also appeared at the festivals. Although the final festival was cancelled due to a flood, the College had increased its reputation and solved its financial difficulties by providing some of the most important performances of the decade.

By the turn of the century, Cincinnati saw the arts as some of the most important features of the city. It was something to display proudly to visitors. As part of the 1910 Cincinnati Industrial Exposition, the city of Cincinnati commissioned the Italian composer and College of Music faculty member Pietro Floridia to compose an opera in commemoration of the occasion. Floridia chose the local artist Paul Jones to write the libretto based on scenes from an unpublished novel entitled *The Sacred Mirror* that Jones had sketched, but not completed. The operatic version would be entitled *Paoletta* after the name of the female lead character.

The premiere on August 29, 1910, at Music Hall was a resounding success. The lead roles were sung by the tenor David Bispham and soprano Bernice de Pasquali, both of whom had sung at the New York Metropolitan Opera. Their understudies were local singers Carl Gantvoort and Edna Showalter. The May Festival Chorus provided 140 singers to create the onstage chorus and 15 dancers traveled from New York to form the *corps de ballet*. The fifty-three-member orchestra was drawn from the Cincinnati Symphony. *Paoletta*'s premiere ended with forty-eight curtain calls, which led to brisk ticket sales for the remaining twenty-eight performances. One of those shows was attended by ex-President Theodore Roosevelt and his daughter, Alice, and son-in-law, Nicholas Longworth.[5]

With the founding of the Cincinnati Opera in 1920, a local chorus was assembled to serve the needs of the company. However, unreasonable expectations were placed upon the singers. Before the season began, each chorister was expected to attend rehearsals four times a week from late March until mid-June. There were seven rehearsals during the last week of preparation. Chorus members received no pay for any of the rehearsals or the first week of performances. The most that a chorister could hope to make during the summer was $15.75 for over sixty rehearsals and six weeks of performances.[6] Between 1926 and 1934, a local chorus was used, but in the late 1920s the ranks of Cincinnati singers were supplemented by others from Chicago. From 1935 to 1955, the Cincinnati Opera employed the New York Metropolitan Opera Chorus and no local singers were used. Since 1956 local singers have appeared in the chorus every year.[7]

The "Giulietta Act" of Jacques Offenbach's *The Tales of Hoffmann* at Cincinnati Opera in 2006. Middle: The last act of Verdi's *Un ballo in maschera* at Cincinnati Opera in 2006. Bottom: The celebratory finale of Richard Wagner's *Die Meistersinger von Nürnberg* at Cincinnati Opera in 2010. (Courtesy of Philip Groshong)

1. Larry Wolz, "Opera in Cincinnati: The Years before the Zoo, 1801-1920" (PhD dissertation, University of Cincinnati, 1983), 18-22.
2. Ibid., 25-26.
3. Ibid., 48-49.
4. Ibid., 142.
5. "Paoletta and the Cincinnati Industrial Exposition of 1910," University of Cincinnati Libraries, http://www.libraries.uc.edu/libraries/arb/archives/collections/Paoletta.html (accessed November 10, 2011).
6. Eldred A. Thierstein, *Cincinnati Opera: From the Zoo to Music Hall* (Hillsdale, Michigan: Deerstone Books, 1995), 4.
7. Ibid., 49.

SingCinnati represented Cincinnati at the 2010 World Choir Games in Shaoxing, China. The Games will take place in Cincinnati in July 2012, the first time they have come to the United States. (Courtesy of Philip Groshong)

have been led by a number of artistic directors over the years. These include Crafton Beck, John Farrell, Kent Peterson, and Dr. Patrick O. Coyle, who led the chorus for sixteen years. As of 2011, Dr. Casey Hayes of Indiana's Franklin College, formerly the co-director of the New York City Gay Men's Chorus, assumed leadership. Guest artists Lee Roy Reams, Ann Hampton Callaway, Kate Clinton, and Andre Crouch are among the many soloists who have appeared with the Cincinnati Men's Chorus over the years.[97]

CONCLUSION

Music is an important social tool and has exercised a strong influence on the people and the reputation of the city of Cincinnati. In the city's earliest years, citizens sought instruction in singing so they could participate with confidence in church and at social gatherings. Singing societies developed according to English and German traditions. English choruses were devoted to musical excellence, but with less attention to singing's social aspects. With the influx of German immigrants, many men's choruses arose to preserve both their music and their ethnic identity. As these small Maennerchore banded together, a tradition of Saengerfests grew into huge celebrations that continue to occur periodically in designated cities. With the advent of the May Festival as an event exhibiting dual English and German influence, the traditions merged, preserving both the organization and the purpose of the English tradition, but with an emphasis on music by German composers. Several modern institutions have continued to advance these

The May Festival Chorus, the Cincinnati Symphony Orchestra, and distinguished soloists, led by James Conlon, receive a standing ovation from their enthusiastic Music Hall audience. (Courtesy of Philip Groshong)

Supertitles generously underwritten by
The Corbett Foundation

159

NOTES

1. F[rank] E. Tunison, *Presto!: From the Singing School to the May Musical Festival* (Cincinnati: E. H. Beasley, 1888), 8.

2. Charles Theodore Greve, *Centennial History of Cincinnati and Representative Citizens* (Chicago: Biographical Publishing Co., 1904), 915.

3. Charles Frederic Goss, *Cincinnati: The Queen City 1788-1912* (Chicago and Cincinnati: S. J. Clarke, 1912), 2:460.

4. Don Heinrich Tolzmann, *German Heritage Guide to the Greater Cincinnati Area*, 2nd ed. (Milford, OH: Little Miami, 2007), 75.

5. Arthur Mees, *Choirs and Choral Music* (London: John Murray, 1901), 205.

6. Greve, *Centennial History*, 917.

7. Goss, *Cincinnati*, 2:460.

8. Tunison, *Presto!*, 13.

9. Goss, *Cincinnati*, 2:461.

10. Tunison, *Presto!*, 15-21.

11. Greve, *Centennial History*, 920.

12. Goss, *Cincinnati*, 2:464.

13. Mary Edmund Spanhaimer, "Heinrich Ammin Ratterman: German-American Author, Poet, and Historian 1832-1923" (PhD dissertation, The Catholic University of America, 1937), 15; Larry Robert Wolz, "Opera in Cincinnati: The Years before the Zoo, 1801-1920" (PhD dissertation, University of Cincinnati, 1983), 312.

14. Tunison, *Presto!*, 33-34.

15. Ibid., 34.

16. Ibid., 34-35.

17. Ibid., 84-95.

18. Charles R. Hebble and Frank P. Goodwin, *The Citizens Book* (Cincinnati: Stewart, 1916), 57; Don Heinrich Tolzmann, *Cincinnati's German Heritage* (Bowie, MD: Heritage, 1994), 46.

19. Ibid., 40.

20. Goss, *Cincinnati*, 2:466.

21. Ibid., 2:463.

22. Tunison, *Presto!*, 38-39. Rattermann was unaware of the earlier Apollonian Society.

23. Goss, *Cincinnati*, 2:465, 467.

24. Ibid., 2:465.

25. Tunison, *Presto!*, 39.

26. Goss, *Cincinnati*, 2:465-466.

27. Tunison, *Presto!*, 40.

28. Ibid., 40.

29. Don Heinrich Tolzmann, *The German-American Experience* (Amherst, NY: Humanity Books,

30. Ibid., 182.

31. Goss, *Cincinnati*, 2:466.

32. Carl Peltz, "Historical Sketch of the North American Saengerbund." In *Andenken an das Goldene Jubilaeum des Nordamerikanischen Saengerbundes* (Cincinnati: Nord-Amerikanischer Sängerbund, 1899), 8-9.

33. *Nord-Amerikanischer Saengerbund,* http://nasaengerbund.org.

34. Ibid., 9.

35. Thomas L. Schleis, "Balatka, Hans," http://oxfordmusiconline.com (accessed September 28, 2011).

36. Peltz, "Historical Sketch," 9.

37. Ibid., 10.

38. "The Cincinnati Saengerfest: A Great Procession and Reception Concert," *New York Times,* June 12, 1879, http://query.nytimes.com/ (accessed September 15, 2011).

39. John Sullivan Dwight, "Orchestral Concerts," *Dwight's Journal of Music* 37, no. 17 (November 24, 1877), 134.

40. Eugene Luening, "The Art of Singing and Music in America." In *Milwaukee: A Guide to the Cream City, for Visitors and Citizens; Giving a History of the Settlement, Development and Present Importance of the City, with a Chronology of Interesting Events: A Souvenir of the 24th Saengerfest of the N[orth] A[merican] Saengerbund* (Milwaukee: Caspar & Zahn, 1886), 20-21.

41. Ibid., 20.

42. "The Cincinnati Saengerfest: A Great Procession and Reception Concert," *New York Times* June 12, 1879.

43. Ibid.

44. "The North American Saengerbund," *New York Times,* June 9, 1879, http://query.nytimes.com/ (accessed September 18, 2011).

45. Peltz, "Historical Sketch," 12.

46. Ibid.

47. *Cincinnati und sein Deutschthum* (Cincinnati: Queen City, 1901), 186-87.

48. Peltz, "Historical Sketch," 17.

49. Ibid., 17-18.

50. Ibid., 19.

51. Ibid.

52. "Hall Unfinished, No Concert," *New York Times,* June 29, 1899, http://query.nytimes.com/ (accessed October 1, 2011).

53. Ibid.

54. Peltz, "Historical Sketch," 20.

55. "Singers in Cincinnati: North American Saengerbund Gives Its Delayed Concert With Great Success Before 10,000 People," *New York Times*, June 30, 1899, http://query.nytimes.com/ (accessed September 21, 2011).

56. Ibid.

57. Peltz, "Historical Sketch," 51-55.

58. Steven Sunderman, e-mail message to author, September 26, 2011. James Conlon, the Festival's current Music Director, and Robert Porco, its current chorus master, hold the longest tenures in these positions in the Festival's history.

59. Tunison, *Presto!*, 97.

60. Sylvia Kleve Sheblessy, *100 Years of the Cincinnati May Festival* (Cincinnati: privately printed, 1973), 9-11.

61. Goss, *Cincinnati*, 1:246; Sheblessy, *100 Years*, 11-12.

62. *Cincinnati Sings --A Choral History 1788-1988* (Cincinnati: Cincinnati Musical Festival Association, 1988), n. p.

63. Leonie C. Frank, *Musical Life in Early Cincinnati and the Origin of the May Festival* (Cincinnati: Ruter Press, 1932), 23.

64. *Golden Jubilee Saengerfest: Cincinnati 1899* (Cincinnati: n. p., 1988).

65. Rose Angela Boehle, *Maria Longworth: A Biography* (Dayton : Landfall Press, 1990), 59.

66. Cincinnati Musical Festival Association, "Executive Committee Minutes 1872-1873" (Cincinnati: manuscript, 1873), 1, 7, 9.

67. Ibid., 22.

68. Ibid., 13.

69. Theodore Thomas, Letter to George Ward Nichols, January 20, 1873. Cincinnati Musical Festival Assn. Papers, Cincinnati Historical Society.

70. Ibid.

71. Ibid.

72. Theodore Thomas, Letter to C. C. Miller. January 20, 1873. Cincinnati Musical Festival Assn. Papers, Cincinnati Historical Society.

73. "Executive Committee Minutes 1872-1873," 4.

74. Ibid., 29.

75. Samuel D. Carey, "Letter to the Editor." *Cincinnati Enquirer*, May 9, 1873, 4.

76. "The Great Musical Festival," *Cincinnati Commercial*, May 7, 1873, 4.

77. "The Musical Festival," *Cincinnati Daily Gazette*, May 8, 1873, 1.

78. "The Great Musical Festival," *Cincinnati Commercial*, May 8, 1873, 1.

79. Otto Singer is the gentleman who trained the chorus.

80. John Sullivan Dwight, "The Cincinnati Festival: Third Day, May 8." *Dwight's Journal of Music* 33, no. 4 (May 31, 1873): 31-32.

81. "The Morale of the Cincinnati Festival," *Church's Musical Visitor* 2 (June 1873) 1. The Chicago reporter seems unaware that there was a large contingent of singers from outside the Cincinnati area, including several participants from Chicago.

82. "The Musical Festival," *Cincinnati Daily Gazette*, May 7, 1873, 4.

83. Ibid.

84. "Great Chorus of Children Sings in Festival Cantata," *Cincinnati Commercial*, May 5, 1906, 12.

85. "Great Assembly Greets Rendition of Solemn Music," *Cincinnati Commercial*, May 2, 1906, 2.

86. Sheblessy, *100 Years*, 51.

87. "May Festival Timeline," *Cincinnati May Festival*, http://mayfestival.com/timeline.html (accessed September 28, 2011).

88. Ibid.

89. Ibid.

90. Ibid.

91. Gail Stockholm, "For Bernstein Festival Is Great Choral Event," *Cincinnati Enquirer*, May 27, 1973: 2G.

92. "Musica Sacra," *Musica Sacra*, http://musica-sacra org (accessed September 29, 2011).

93. "Cincinnati Camerata: About Us," *Cincinnati Camerata*, http://cincinnaticamerata.com (accessed September 29, 2011).

94. "The Southern Gateway Chorus," *Southern Gateway Chorus*, http:// southerngateway.org (accessed September 29, 2011).

95. "Gala Choruses," *GALA Choruses*, http:// galachoruses.org (accessed September 26, 2011).

96. "MUSE: Cincinnati's Women's Choir," *MUSE*, http:// musechoir.org (accessed September 26, 2011).

97. "Cincinnati Men's Chorus," *Cincinnati Men's Chorus*, http:// cincinnatimenschorus.org (accessed September 26, 2011).

Cincinnati's
AFRICAN AMERICAN
CHORAL TRADITION
1824-2012

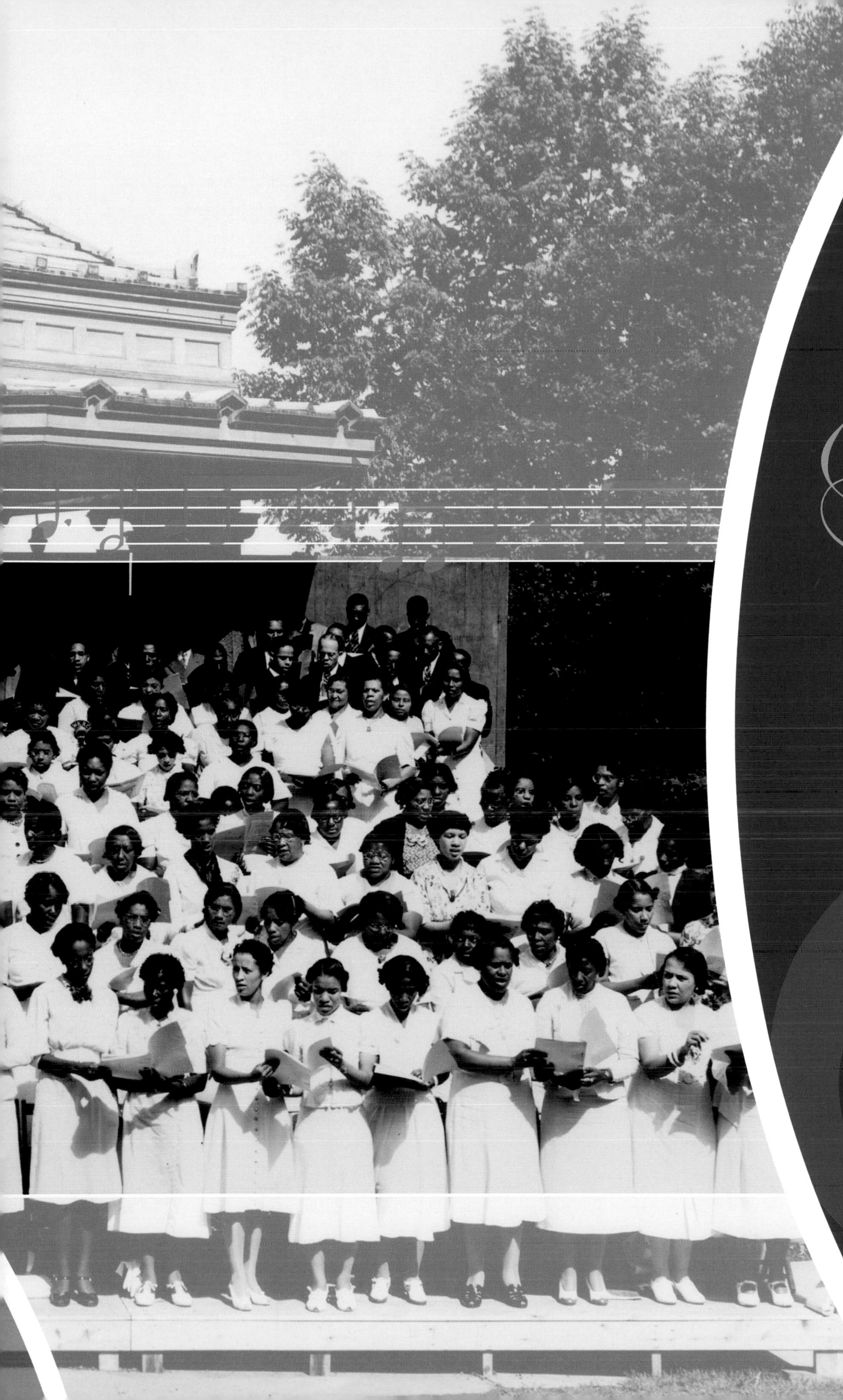

Chapter Four

by Catherine Roma

Throughout the history of African Americans in Cincinnati, choral music and organizations have provided black citizens a major organizational and cultural forum for advocating equality. Whether in churches or civic organizations, blacks created opportunities to sing in a segregated city, and in so doing created an important social force in the city. For example, as early as 1838 the choir, and indeed the entire congregation, of Bethel Church assembled to celebrate in song the British emancipation of enslaved people of the West Indies. For the local celebration of the August holiday the church gathered at midnight to sing "Blow Ye Trumpet, Blow," a Charles Wesley hymn also known as the "Jubilee Hymn."[1] From the beginning, Cincinnati's African American choirs provided a venue for local expression and means to connect the black community to musicians and movements across the country and internationally.

Choirs such as that of Bethel Church provide a unique angle for understanding the black community. In Cincinnati, early in the nineteenth century, black people organized independent churches, and singing was integral to the mission of these autonomous organizations. The church venue provided a space to build community with leaders of their own choice, a place where collective deliverance and redemption were expressed in word and song. By the 1830s Cincinnati's progressive urban churches introduced choral singing into their services. One could hear psalms, hymns, and anthems sung at Allen Temple African Methodist Episcopal Church (the renamed Bethel, mentioned above) and African Union Baptist Church.

In 1921, Artie Matthews founded the Cosmopolitan School of Music in Cincinnati, the first black-owned and operated conservatory in the United States. In a segregated society, Matthews established a viable independent and autonomous institution where African Americans, excluded from Cincinnati's Conservatory of Music and the College of Music, were afforded the opportunity to study with trained black musicians. Though no choir was associated with the Cosmopolitan School, Matthews took advantage of every opportunity to conduct community choirs, through Cincinnati's emerging municipal public recreation program, which led in training black choral singers throughout the city.

Through the efforts of Cincinnati Recreation Commission's Department of Colored Work, the first June Festival was held in 1938. Since the prestigious May Festival did not welcome blacks until 1956, the June Festival served to bring together nationally recognized black soloists and conductors to perform in concert with a large community choir that met year round to hone their skills as trained choral musicians. As a result of blacks' increased opportunities for participation and interest in choral music, independent black ensembles were formed in the 1940s and continue today.

EARLY HISTORY

The documented history of arts activities in the African American community in nineteenth-century Cincinnati is sparse, seemingly neglected, and leaves substantial room for research. While some important events are recorded, there is no comprehensive chronicle of the choral arts of the city's African Americans.

W. P. Dabney's *Cincinnati's Colored Citizens* and Lyle Koehler's *Cincinnati's Black People*[2] cite invaluable firsts and short biographical sketches of important people. Nikki M. Taylor, in her *Frontiers of Freedom,* provides historical data, previously lacking, in the fields of social and political history when she "examines the process by which a transient population of former slaves developed into a self-conscious black community."[3] However, no published source reveals the vital part that music, particularly choral music, played in the cultural life of African Americans in Cincinnati in the nineteenth century.

Taylor posits that Cincinnati had a complex blend of identities as a city. Situated above the Mason-Dixon line, hence a northern town, it was nevertheless southern in its political and economic outlook, and western in its commercial aspirations.[4] Similarly, Gina Ruffin Moore describes Cincinnati as "a Northern City with a Southern Exposure." This mix of characteristics shaped life for the city's African Americans, whose presence was essentially unwelcome. The first of Ohio's Black Laws, passed in 1804, were intended to restrict the migration of fugitive slaves into Ohio. According to census data from 1801, there were 337 blacks in Ohio, but none in Cincinnati. By 1810, eighty of Ohio's 1,890 blacks lived in Cincinnati, and the black population continued to grow, reaching 2,255 by 1840.[5]

Racial and ethnic hierarchies had already begun to develop in Cincinnati before this time. At the top were native-born Protestant whites and English immigrants. Below them were the Germans, and even further down the list were the Irish. African Americans occupied the bottom layer. This ethnic stratification led to occupational stratification for many as well, including blacks. Some blacks chose to leave Cincinnati due to its unfriendly climate, seeking to escape the city's violent riots and discriminatory regulations, such as the one requiring blacks to pay bond if they wanted to stay in the city.[6]

For blacks who remained, though under difficult and oppressive conditions, there were certain kinds of jobs available. At first, they were employed as day laborers, barbers, and menial servants. Later, they were able to get jobs at the riverfront as stewards and on cabin crews. Hotels employed waiters and men worked in stores, factories, and coal yards. In addition, a significant number of black Cincinnatians stayed in the city and worked to purchase loved ones from slavery.[7] Indeed, Cincinnati hummed with activity as a vital stop on the Underground Railroad. Runaway slaves were assisted primarily by the city's free blacks, although networks of cooperative black and white communities worked together to provide passage, protection, and safe haven. Many times the cooperation of the entire network was needed to move one slave through Cincinnati to freedom. White abolitionist Levi Coffin, a Quaker often called the President of the Underground Railroad, persuaded some whites to join the freedom band. Prominent citizens Salmon P. Chase,

James Birney, and Gamaliel Bailey all harbored slaves in the 1830s.[8]

The resilience and resolve of Cincinnati's black citizens led them to create meaningful institutions for mutual survival and renewal. Early in the nineteenth century the black church provided an important safe haven, where African Americans found acceptance and the freedom to create their own forms of independent and autonomous worship. In 1824, black members of the Methodist Episcopal Deer Creek Church applied for admission to the African Methodist Church, the first black religious denomination, founded in Philadelphia in 1816 by Richard Allen (1760-1831). Allen Temple African Methodist Episcopal Church (AME), named after Allen's church in Philadelphia, is the oldest black church in Cincinnati. Because Allen felt singing to be of vital importance in the service, one of his initial acts as minister was to compile a hymnal, the first hymn book by a black man, for use by a black congregation. Eileen Southern observes, "Allen's hymnal is apparently the earliest source in history that includes hymns to which wandering choruses or refrains are attached, that is, choruses that are freely added to any hymn rather than affixed permanently to specific hymns." She adds that "many of these hymns served as source material for the spirituals of the slaves—the so-called Negro spirituals."[9]

To this day Allen Temple is a leader in choral music, and has been instrumental in developing the Classical Roots Concerts and *Opera Goes to Church*, beloved programs appreciated by all of Cincinnati. Dr. Robert Gazaway, the Minister of Music at Allen Temple for the last eighteen years, conducts the Sanctuary, Allegro Adult Mass Choir, and the Shelby Walker Male Chorus. He notes that many trained, well-known musicians have served at the church during its long history.[10]

Allen Temple African Methodist Episcopal Church, 1870, previously a Jewish synagogue.

In 1831, seven years after the founding of the AME church in Cincinnati, the first Negro Baptist church, African Union Baptist Church, was formed. In 1842, Zion Baptist Church was organized and was active in the Underground Railroad. Mt. Zion Baptist Church was founded in 1869. Both Zion Baptist and Mt. Zion Baptist separated from Union Baptist to form their own, independent churches in Lockland and Avondale, respectively. All three churches continue today with vibrant choral programs, committed to performing the diversity of genres available to them: spirituals, anthems, classical music by both black and white composers, and gospel music.[11]

On April 8, 1842, the Singing Five, a group at Union Baptist, applied to use the church basement to teach singing. The church granted their request and, after much discussion, passed a resolution permitting the group to use instruments. Later that year, by a very close vote, the church authorized a choir for their worship services. "It was a difficult task to bring the church around to the need of a church choir of male and female voices.... To become a member of the choir, it was necessary to attend the [church's] school of music."[12] In 1864, at the dedication of Union Baptist Church's new church building, it was noted:

"Amid all this show and pageantry are the solid men and women of the community.... Leading the choir in the gallery, is seen the intellectual head of Cincinnati's most accomplished musician, and graceful and poignant writer, Joseph C. Corbin, keeping time with the sweet-sounding notes of the melodeon;[13] which is discoursing most eloquent music."[14]

Less than a year later, *The Christian Recorder* noted:

"Allen Temple has both a melodeon in its Sabbath School and a grand organ.... We can find no impropriety in introducing instrumental music into our churches, where the people are prepared for it. Let all of our members purchase hymn books and learn to sing in the choir in the proper manner."[15] This early emphasis on musical training and singing at Allen Temple is noteworthy. The importance of congregational hymn singing and choral participation illustrates the value placed on music throughout the service.

By 1850, Cincinnati was the sixth largest city in the United States, having a population of more than 115,000. Its black population of 3,237 constituted one of the ten largest free black communities in antebellum America. During this period descriptions of the distinctive religious songs of the blacks became more common. Musicologist Dena Epstein records that on the afternoon of November 27, 1850, Fredrika Bremer visited an African Methodist Church in Cincinnati and remarked:

"I found in the African Church African ardor and African life. The church was full to overflowing, and the congregation sang their own hymns. The singing ascended and poured forth like a melodious torrent, and the heads feet and elbows of the congregation moved all in unison with it, amid evident enchantment and delight in the singing.... The hymns and psalms which the Negros have themselves composed have a peculiar naïve character, childlike, full of imagery and life."[16]

While the characterization of the

Steal Away.

Steal a-way, steal a-way, steal a-way to Je-sus!

Steal a-way, steal a-way home, I hain't got long to stay here.

1. My Lord calls me, He calls me by the thunder; The
2. Green trees are bending, Poor sin-ners stand trembling; The,&c.

trumpet sounds it in my soul: I hain't got long to stay here.

choir's songs as "naïve" and "childlike" may sound pejorative to contemporary ears, it is nonetheless clear that black music, and particularly the Negro spiritual, was gaining a place in the public consciousness.

THE FISK JUBILEE SINGERS

The Fisk Jubilee Singers helped to establish the spiritual as an art form. This ensemble from Nashville, Tennessee, embarked on a tour in October 1871 that would follow the old Underground Railroad stations, stopping at abolitionist houses and churches from Ohio through the Mid-Atlantic and New England States, to earn money for their home institution, Fisk University, which was then in deep financial trouble. George White and his

Top left: Arrangement of "Steal Away" from G. D. Pike's *Jubilee Singers* (1873) by Ella Sheppard. 1871 portrait of the nine-member Jubilee Singers. (Fisk University Franklin Library Special Collections) The group toured extensively in the USA and abroad. Opposite page left to right: George Leonard White, treasurer of Fisk University, whose first passion was music, founded Jubilee Singers, felt chosen by God to save Fisk from financial woes. Ella Sheppard, first black hired at Fisk by White. Singer Maggie Porter, soprano, was one of the Jubilee Singers.

nine black singers, all but one of them former slaves, left Nashville by train and traveled to Cincinnati.[17] In 1868 White had hired Ella Sheppard, a capable music student at Fisk who served as assistant conductor and vocal coach of the group and played piano. She was the first black hired by the institution.[18] G. D. Pike's 1873 account of the journey to Cincinnati is revealing:

"On reaching the depot, though holding first-class tickets, they were shown into a caboose car, or as one of them styled it, a chicken box; and in this way they rode through the day, reaching Cincinnati in the evening. Here they found lodging in a colored boarding house; and the next day, Saturday, visited the Exposition, which at the time, was attracting a large amount of visitors. On reaching the musical department, Professor White requested Miss Sheppard to play 'Annie Laurie,' with variations upon the piano. Almost at once a crowd gathered, and exclamations were heard on all sides, 'Only see! She's a nigger.' 'Do you see that?' 'Do you hear that? Why she's a nigger.' On being invited to sing, the troupe gave 'The Spangled Banner,' with 'Red, White and Blue,' 'Away to the Meadows,' and other favorites, every note seeming to increase the crowd, till it became so great one could scarcely tell where it commenced. Wherever the Singers moved the crowd followed, with an admiration entirely new to these people, who, for many years, had no rights a white man was bound to respect."[19]

The next evening, local Congregational ministers Reverends Halley and Moore met with White, listened to several sacred selections by his ensemble, and "were so pleased that they decided at once to hold praise meetings the next day, to afford the people opportunity to listen to their songs."[20] The singers gave several performances in Cincinnati and in nearby towns over the next few days, drawing sizable crowds and positive praise, but failing to receive offerings sufficient to offset their expenses.

On their return visit a short while later, the

attend white schools; yet even so, the color line remained. By 1920, 31.9 percent of Cincinnati's black population (30,079) lived in the city's very crowded West End. A steady influx of disenfranchised southern blacks arrived in the city in 1917, driven by the continuing economic inequalities and discrimination. It was not the increasing population that was problematic, however, but the color line itself. As Tracy notes:

"The problem of the twentieth century, in Cincinnati as elsewhere, was, as W.E.B. Du Bois proclaimed, the problem of the color line, and out of such eighteenth- and nineteenth-century backgrounds and that twentieth- century milieu emerged the blues musicians who distinguished Cincinnati's street corners, speakeasies, bars, nightclubs, record players, radios and televisions with their music—not of the middle but of the lower class."[35]

The color line notwithstanding, black music grew and flourished in Cincinnati. Singer Mamie Smith (1883-1946), born in Cincinnati, was the first black to record a solo blues record, "Crazy Blues," for the race recording label Okeh Record Co. in 1920.

At about the same time, Artie Matthews's arrival in Cincinnati was to change the course of events for many African Americans. Celebrated across the Midwest as an important ragtime composer, performer, and arranger, equal to the nationally recognized Scott Joplin, Matthews was considered the best sight reader of all the pianists in the St. Louis area. His advanced compositional style, seen in his five published *Pastime* rags, foreshadows later jazz piano styles.[36] Matthews came to Cincinnati to accept a job at St. Andrews Episcopal Church as organist and choir master, and to study organ and music theory at the Metropolitan College of Music, Elocution, and Drama. Beginning with Matthews's tenure, St. Andrews Episcopal Church has been known as one of the black churches in Cincinnati with a continuing commitment to perform traditional classical music. In an interview, Irma Tillery spoke of the rich musical history of St. Andrews, from the time the church was located Downtown at Eighth and Mound

Artie Matthews, founder of Cosmopolitan School of Music.

Streets. She spoke highly of her predecessors, including Helen Greer, a junior high choral music teacher at the Harriet Beecher Stowe School, who trained at the Cosmopolitan School. Dr. Newell Fitzpatrick, a classically trained musician who frequently performed the choral works of his favorites, Handel and Mendelssohn, followed Greer in 1951. Ms. Tillery, a trained pianist, studied privately from an early age with Abraham Gerskiwitz, her teacher at Bloom Junior High School. She was on the editorial board of *Lift Every Voice and Sing,* the black Episcopal hymnal in which she has two arrangements—"Oh! What a Beautiful City" and "Joshua Fit de Battle of Jericho"— and one original composition, "O Lord, How Perfect Is Your Name."

Artie Matthews met Anna Howard, his wife-to-be, at the Metropolitan School, and together they founded the Cosmopolitan School of Music at 823 W. Ninth Street in 1921. Because the doors of the Cincinnati Conservatory of Music were closed to aspiring African American musicians, as were those of the College of Music of Cincinnati, Matthews's Cosmopolitan School provided advanced educational and musical opportunities for African Americans. He sought to bring equity to a discriminatory system through the establishment of the school, which became the first black-owned and operated conservatory in the United States.[37]

Matthews himself had studied choral conducting under Frank Van der Stucken, former conductor of the Cincinnati Symphony Orchestra (1905-1912, 1925-1929), and arranged music for the orchestra. At the Cosmopolitan

School he taught organ, piano, and music theory, as well as orchestration. He directed the senior choir at Calvary Methodist Church from 1938 until his death in 1958.[38] In 1938 Matthews received an honorary Doctor of Music degree from Ohio's Wilberforce University.

The curriculum at the Cosmopolitan School included languages, expression, public school music, theory, violin, voice, piano, organ, band, orchestra, chamber ensemble, and natural dancing. The school was an officially accredited school of music and awarded certificates and diplomas. The *Cincinnati Post* reported that the Race Relations Committee of the Women's City Club met at the school once per year, and committee members Mrs. Albert Roth, Mrs. William Hegner, and Mrs. Ralph Oesper showed a keen interest in the success of the school. Through their contacts they persisted in securing accreditation for the school, calling on Dean L. A. Pechstein and Dr. Gordon Hendrickson of Teachers College at the University of Cincinnati for support.[39]

M. Ruth Brown Phillips, who studied at the Cosmopolitan School, recalled that no teachers from either the College of Music or the Conservatory of Music taught at Cosmopolitan. Phillips was emphatic that the exams the Conservatory faculty came to administer at the end of

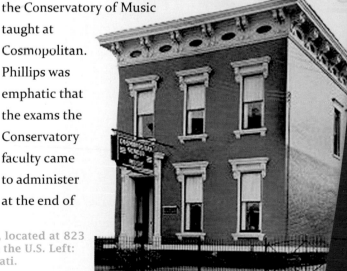

The Cosmopolitan School of Music, founded in 1921, located at 823 W. 9th St., was the first black-owned conservatory in the U.S. Left: Mamie Smith, blues recording artist, born in Cincinnati.

every semester were the same as those given to students at the Conservatory. She remembers:

"Dr. Artie Matthews was my piano teacher, and he taught orchestration. You know, we couldn't go to the Conservatory College, so we took everything that was required, musically speaking, and they (the faculty at the Conservatory) would come down and give us exams. They'd come down there—you know, they don't know the person, they don't know you, if you flunked the test, that was it. That's a whole year's work down the drain."[40]

Edna Virgil (nee Edna Catherine Anderson) was born in the West End, graduated from Woodward High School, and attended the University of Cincinnati, aspiring to be a concert pianist, but was not able to study at the Conservatory. She taught voice at the Cosmopolitan School of Music, coached choral groups there, and worked with the Cincinnati Recreation music department. She was Minister of Music for ten years at Calvary Methodist Church, conducting the choir and playing organ. She was a singing member of the University of Cincinnati Singers, and in 1932 was president of the organization. Another important member of the voice faculty at Cosmopolitan was William T. Gee. He was organist and choir director at Calvary Baptist Church and later succeeded Matthews as organist and choir director at Calvary Methodist Church.

Artie Matthews's musical talents and ingenuity lay not only in his critical role in providing a level playing field for African Americans who wished to further their musical education, and in training fine choirs at his church, but also in creating outlets for community music making in Cincinnati.

THE ROLE OF THE CINCINNATI RECREATION COMMISSION

Across the country, starting in the 1920s, municipal public recreation organizations played pivotal roles in establishing public recreation programs. Cincinnati was one city among many that benefited from these activities, which improved race relations and highlighted the importance of participatory community music. James Hathaway Robinson, a Yale-educated African American sociologist and local social worker, studied the needs of Cincinnati's black citizens for the Negro Civic Welfare Association, and recommended the creation of a new agency "devoted to community music and education" for the black community. Prompted by Robinson's continued calls for new programs, Cincinnati Community Service created a Department of Negro Recreation in 1922. Their programs included athletic events, community sings, and a city-wide "Colored Orchestra."[41]

The Cincinnati Recreation Commission notes in the Report of the Department of Colored Work, 1930: "Another new and successful activity was the Community Choral Club, organized and conducted by Artie Matthews.... Sixty-five members were enrolled and a Choral Club Concert presented at the end of the season. Competent critics acclaimed the concert as one of exceptional merit."[42] By 1932 the Choral Club had grown to eighty members and performed five concerts that year.[43]

On Saturday afternoon, June 24, 1933, the annual report of the Public Recreation Commission recorded a concert presented by "a chorus of 400 adults and 312 children... with an audience of 5,000 to 6,000 looking on... J. Wesley Jones,[44] executive secretary of the National Association of Negro Musicians, an eminent choral leader from Chicago, was the Guest Conductor."[45] In addition to the establishment of the Community Choral Club, other significant musical activities were established. Interest in community choral work in Cincinnati is described in an article in the *Yearbook of the Music Educators National Conference* of 1934, where a full section is dedicated to the city's community music program. According to this report, "Adult choruses enrolled 1,340 singers and had 210 rehearsals; and children's choruses had 30 rehearsals with 312 participants. The community sings involved 49,800 singers."[46] The report also noted:

"During the past two years we have instituted an extended program of choral music among our colored citizens. These choruses range from informal groups, which confine themselves to spirituals and other folk tunes, on through choruses of fair ability to a group of selected voices called an Artist Chorus."[47]

In 1935 the Recreation Commission reported a concert "by the combined Negro Choruses in April at Hughes High School."[48]

Looking back at this era, Donald Spencer, in written reminiscences, reflected on his time at the University of Cincinnati.

"There were no black students in any of the extracurricular activities, and there were none in the student government. That was 1932.... We were determined to change things; we would not settle for 'no sociability, no involvement in college activities.' We organized a group and named it QUADRES. We decided we did not just want to sing spirituals, we wanted to give a musical comedy. I wrote 13 or 14 musical numbers that we used, and we called the musical 'Who'da Thought It.' We had an orchestra of about 16 pieces. It was performed in Wilson Auditorium in May 1933. QUADRES became a strong campus organization."[49]

R. Nathaniel Dett, music director at the Negro College for Women in Greensboro, North Carolina, brought a chorus of fifty black women to Cincinnati to perform at Calvary Methodist Church on October 7, 1938.[50] In 1939, black civic, religious, and educational groups sponsored the presentation of *Jacob's Ladder*, a musical pageant, at Emery Auditorium to celebrate the 75th anniversary of the Emancipation Proclamation. With a cast of 250, this performance depicted "the struggle of the American Negro." Arthur D. Williams, pastor at Mt. Zion Church, wrote the play while he was a postgraduate student at Yale University. It elicited

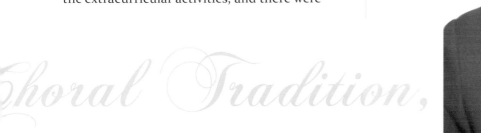

Donald Spencer, one of 125 black students out of 11,000 at the University of Cincinnati in 1932, created extracurricular activities for black students, including QUADRES.

high praise from critics. The anniversary of the Emancipation Proclamation was also celebrated by radio station WCPO, which scheduled broadcasts of black speakers and singers.[51]

THE JUNE FESTIVAL

In 1938 what was to become known as the June Festival solidified with the success of the Negro Folk Song Festival directed by Dr. Clarence Cameron White. The festival was held at the Eden Park Bandstand, where an audience of 4,000 listened to a chorus of 243 voices. Again in 1939 Dr. White returned to train 300 singers and conduct the performance in June. The Public Recreation Department reported: "Unquestionably, the outstanding single event of the year was the Annual June Festival of Negro Music, not so much because of the improved quality of performances and the increase in paid attendance, but rather because of definite strides made in the direction of a permanent organization."[52]

The much sought-after Clarence Cameron White was a member of a group of African American artists and intellectuals who came to the fore during the Harlem Renaissance of the 1920s and 1930s. White learned violin at an early age and later attended Oberlin Conservatory of Music (1896-1901). He studied composition in Europe with Samuel Taylor Coleridge, among others, and taught at the Washington (DC) Conservatory of Music (1903-1907). He toured extensively as a violinist, accompanied on piano by his wife Beatrice Warrick White. Recognized as a gifted composer, especially inspired by the spirituals, he wrote in a style considered "neo-Romantic and flavored with black American folk idioms."[53] He was

the artistic director of the Victorian Concert Orchestra in Boston (1914-1920), and followed R. Nathaniel Dett as conductor of the Hampton Institute Choir in 1933.

In 1939 the Cincinnati Recreation Commission decided to make the previously ad hoc June Festival of Negro Music a permanent annual event. The advisory council for this initiative included many of the same people who had supported the accreditation of the Cosmopolitan School of Music. Among the black and white Cincinnatians who helped draft the charter for the Festival Association were Dr. L. A. Pechstein, Dean of the College of Education at the University of Cincinnati, and Mrs. Albert S. Roth, a Past President of the Women's City Club. The June Festival Association was organized "for the purpose of furthering opportunity for musical expression among Negro citizens of Cincinnati."[54] Dr. White traveled to Cincinnati in May to mold the singers "from community choruses, glee clubs and gospel choirs into one great song group which will present a program of classical music and traditional spirituals."[55]

In an unpublished interview conducted in 2005 by Janelle Gelfand, Arthur Herndon, a Cincinnati-born operatic tenor of international reputation, reminds us that "many people have forgotten about the June Festival and the fact that it was a supplement at the time for the May Festival. So it [the June Festival] was organized for those of us who were classically trained." The May Festival Chorus opened its membership to African Americans only in 1956.

The increased success, participation, and interest in classical singing caused the June Festival Chorus to rehearse on a regular basis. In

Top: The June Festival Chorus, Eden Park, June 4, 1939. (Courtesy of Cincinnati Historical Society)
Bottom: Clarence Cameron White, conductor, accomplished composer and violinist.

1940, rather than the short four week rehearsal schedule prior to their June performances, the group began to rehearse on Monday nights in February at the Stowe School. Dr. Artie Matthews prepared the festival chorus, and Mr. Clinton Gibbs was the accompanist. By 1941 the choir held regular rehearsals year round. The ages of the chorus members ranged from 17 to 100. In planning for one of the most memorable performances of the June Festival, Harry Glore, secretary and business manager of the June Festival Association, said, "We feel that the race that gave to the world of music such superb artists as Marian Anderson, Paul Robeson, and Dorothy Maynor, ought to have a real opportunity to make its contribution to this city's cultural life."[56]

So it was. On June 18, 1942, Paul Robeson appeared with 300 singers at the fifth annual June Festival, held at 8:15 p.m. at Crosley Field. Earl Robinson's *Ballad for Americans*, a patriotic cantata, featured Robeson's powerful baritone voice, and was the centerpiece of the program. Other works included in the concert, attended by over 7,000 on a very rainy evening, featured Robeson in "Bless This House," "The Glory Road," the Death Scene from the opera *Boris Godunov*, and "Ol' Man River."

A 200-voice children's chorus from the Cincinnati Public Schools sang at the June Festival in 1945, when it was held on the campus of the University of Cincinnati. In 1948 the June Festival took place at the Cincinnati Zoo. The highly respected and renowned baritone Todd Duncan (the original Porgy in *Porgy and Bess*) sang and John W.

Pictures from left to right: Paul Robeson, June Festival, 1942 (Copyright Billy Rose Theatre Division, New York Public Library for the Performing Arts). June Festival rehearsal, Harriet Beecher Stowe School, 1938, Dr. White, conductor. Todd Duncan performed at the June Festival, 1945 (Billy Rose Theatre Div. NYPL/PA). June Festival rehearsal, May 3, 1940, Stowe School. Audience, Eden Park, June Festival, 1947.

City of Cincinnati

PUBLIC RECREATION COMMISSION
ROOM 114 · CITY HALL

TAM DEERING
DIRECTOR OF RECREATION

October 13, 1941

COMMISSION
MAX HIRSCH, President
EDWIN G. BECKER
FREDERICK W. HINKLE
W. O. RAKESTRAW
MRS. URBAN C. VARNAU

SUPERVISORS
ATHLETICS
    CHARLES SHEAR
COLORED WORK
    DEHART HUBBARD
    MRS. ETHEL R. CLARK
COMMUNITY ACTIVITIES
    MABEL MADDEN
GOLF
    ROBERT J. STRAUSS
MUSIC
    HARRY F. GLORE
PLAYGROUNDS
    ROBERT E. COADY
TENNIS
    CHAS. R. TRAVIS

n Kems: This will give you the essential facts for a newsitem — Thank you — HG.

Dear Friends:

You are familiar with the amazing growth of the annual June Festival of Negro Music. This year we are going further; we are getting a big-time soloist. Nogotiations are under way for Paul Robeson. If he is not available then we will try Anderson, Maynor, or Hayes — — the point is our soloist will be the best available. Interest has grown to such a peak we are giving the next festival at Crosley Field.

We are anxious to raise the standard of our chorus by adding the best singers in Cincinnati who are not now members. Will you help us? We are launching a membership campaign. Application for membership may be filed at the studios of Dr. Artie Matthews, 823 W. 9th St. PA-9868 or Mr. Clinton Gibbs, 2819 Preston Ave., WO-4175.

Sincerely,

Harry Glore

Secretary

181

Two views of the Excelsior Singers (1942). Many important male singers, directors, and accompanists were part of their rich history.

Music at First Antioch Baptist Church. In April, 1942, The James V. Roach Excelsior Singers became a reality. Under the short tenure of the next director, George Colin, the group changed its name to The Excelsior Singers. Richard E. Bush, a leading tenor in the group, next assumed the role of director. For a short time, David F. Brown directed. Finally, the accompanist for the group, William B. Crooms (1914-2010), assumed the accompanist-director role. A concert program of 1992 defined the group's goals.

"The aim of this group is to perform good sacred and secular music. The singing of the Excelsiors far and wide serves as a vehicle through which music communicates the brotherhood of mankind. The music performed by The Excelsior Singers transcends the boundaries of all religions and underscores the universality of the human soul."[62]

Staples of their repertoire included music by Handel and Mozart, arranged spirituals, sacred works by contemporary black composers, and occasionally, music from popular musicals of the day. According to John Bailey and Herbert Mitchell, members of The Excelsiors, the group did not sing much gospel music.

Bailey and Mitchell also spoke extensively about their choral training in public schools and in church. John Bailey studied voice with Professor William T. Gee, then choir director at Calvary Baptist Church and voice teacher at the Cosmopolitan School. Herbert Mitchell remembers that James V. Roach "kind of organized people from my church choir to sing with some more groups of us, other city choirs." Mitchell remembers Roach as a director who "was very determined to

get his point over, and you went over it until you got it down." He also recalls joining The Excelsiors in 1947 "right after I was in high school." John Bailey remarked that he had joined The Excelsiors later because "I was singing with William Gee. William Gee had an octet called The Cavaliers, [and] I was singing with that group" [as a first baritone]. Also in the Cavaliers were Clyde Williams,[63] who sang second tenor, and Wade Mann, who sang second bass.

Daphne Robinson notes that William T. Gee's interest in classical sacred music led him to organize a volunteer choir comprised of people from several local churches. This choir stayed together for at least ten years, rehearsing every Sunday afternoon from early fall, to perform on Palm Sunday.[64] John Bailey also spoke of Gee.

"...as director of our senior choir [at Calvary Baptist], you know, every Palm Sunday, it was traditional to get a group of people from other parts of the city, and augment our choir, and give either a cantata—we sang a *Stabat Mater* once—and also Verdi's *Requiem.* He'd have the choir around him, he'd be in the middle, and he would play and direct the choir."[65]

John Bailey recalls "we took music, we were in the choir, at Woodward, we had a choir bell every day and learned how to read, read music.... The choirs were pretty strong there, that's where we learned our appreciation for music."[66] Memorable music teachers from Bailey's years at Harriet Beecher Stowe School were Helen Greer, previously mentioned, and Charles Keys. Mable McCallahan taught Glondora Moore voice and piano.

The Baroque Choral Ensemble (BCE)

was founded in 1968 by Richard Bush, then director of the *a cappella* choir at St. John AME Zion Church. The BCE grew out of the church's mixed SATB choir to become an independent, nonprofit choral organization. Its members included

"...men and women of diverse religious philosophies, professional and laymen, accomplished musicians and novices; all gather[ed] with a unity of purpose: to strive relentlessly to obtain the pinnacle of perfection in our performances of secular and sacred music. We have dedicated ourselves to the preservation of the Negro Spirituals as an art form."[67]

Richard E. Bush, the founder and director of the Baroque Choral Ensemble, graduated from Walnut Hills High School, where he played first violin in the school orchestra. He served as choral director at St. John AME Zion Church and the Trinity Missionary Baptist Church, and was director of the James V. Roach Excelsior men's ensemble. After completing his doctorate (DMA) in choral conducting at the University of Cincinnati's College-Conservatory of Music, Dr. Bush performed extensively as a tenor soloist in New York, Chicago, Washington, DC, and New Orleans. He arranged the music for and sang with the Gospel Reporters Quartette throughout the South and Midwest, and arranged many of the well-loved spirituals performed by the BCE.

The BCE performed throughout the greater Tristate region, sang in concert with the Cincinnati Symphony Orchestra, and traveled to Washington, DC to perform at Turner Memorial AME Church (including

Pictures from left to right: kneeling, William B. Crooms (L), and Richard E. Bush (R) in front of members of the Baroque Choral Ensemble. Middle pictures are of the Spirimelodaires from Union Baptist Church, begun in 1961, and most recently directed by Ruth Brown Phillips. Far right: Richard E. Bush, in black suit, with members of early Baroque Ensemble from St. John's AME Zion.

Cincinnati's African American

THE CARMEL PRESBYTERIAN CHURCH

DR. B. B. EVANS, MINISTER

AND

ST. JOHN A. M. E. ZION CHURCH

DR. J. F. DUNN, MINISTER

present

A CHRISTMAS PORTION

of

"The Messiah"

by

George Fredrick Handel

Sunday, December 20, 1959

5:00 P. M.

—at—

CARMEL PRESBYTERIAN CHURCH

Reading Road at Lee Place

Cincinnati 29, Ohio

SOLOISTS

ANN GREENE, Soprano   JUANITA GIBSON, Contralto

RICHARD E. BUSH, Tenor   ROBERT GREENE, Bass

Loretta Manggrum's complete compositional output is housed in the Library of Congress. Her collection represents the country's first generation of black composers who wrote for the concert stage. An accomplished pianist, Manggrum played in churches and for silent movies.

a performance for the White House staff). The group also took part in the Appalachian Festival in Ashland, Kentucky, and the Festival of Lights on Fountain Square in Cincinnati. The Baroques sponsored a college scholarship fund for aspiring young musicians. One of Ann Greene's most cherished memories was of Erich Kunzel coming to a church basement to rehearse excerpts from *Porgy and Bess* and James Furman's *I Have a Dream,* performed in 1971 with the Baroque Choral Ensemble.[68]

Referring to the commitment and abilities of the singers in the ensemble, Ann Greene said: "Those people could read music, they could sing, they could watch every gesture.... There was a love, a love that they had for the music."[69] She remembered the time early in the ensemble's history when Judge Nathaniel Jones approached her after the concert and, overcome with the performance, said, "It did my soul good, I didn't know there were groups like this who did those spirituals like that any more."[70]

Another member of the BCE recalled, "The group had a unique sound because it was made up of mothers and daughters, sisters and brothers, husbands and wives, most of whom were excellent soloists in their own right but knew how to blend well with the group."[71] Ann Greene, a charter member of the group,

emphatically stated:

"Many people don't know our black musicians, but these were people who studied, who had degrees. Anyway, they all—what we all had in common was we could not attend the College of Music…. We wanted to learn, and we didn't care where we were as long as we had good teachers, and they sent good teachers down to us [from the College-Conservatory of Music (CCM) to the Cosmopolitan School]. Some of us were able to finish, others were not. I know Johanna [Byrd] and I both had to drop out because of financial difficulties, but Richard Bush finally went on through."[72]

In 1971, the Cincinnati Symphony Orchestra, under the direction of Erich Kunzel, performed the world premiere of James Furman's *I Have a Dream.* The symphonic oratorio featured local soprano soloist Lois Wilkins as Gospel Soloist II and McHenry Boatwright as the voice of Dr. Martin Luther King. Choral forces included the Baroque Choral Ensemble (Richard Bush, conductor), Central State University Chorus (Steven Glenn, conductor), Kentucky State College Chapel Choir (Carl H. Smith, conductor), and Wilberforce University Choir (Robert Alexander, conductor). Local musicians Geneva Kinard (gospel piano) and Cal Collins (banjo) also performed. The composer, James Furman

EXCERPTS FROM A LETTER WRITTEN TO COMPOSER APRIL 14, 1958.

"Your Cantata is truly a brilliant achievement and deserves the attention of Choral Groups throughout the Nation, capable of meeting its technical demands."

It is with great regret that I shall not be here on June 6th to enjoy its premiere which I am sure will be a splendid musical and spiritual experience for those attending and performing, as well as a triumph for you."

THOR JOHNSON

Premiere Presentation
of Canta — BEHOLD

SUNDAY, JANUARY 5, 1969   4:00

FIRST CHURCH OF GOD
230 Fosdic & Bellevue

SECOND PERFORMANCE, JANUARY 1

5:00 P.M.

ST. JOHN A.M.E. ZION CHURCH

(1937-1989), a native of Kentucky, was also a conductor and professor of music at Western Connecticut State University in Danbury. He intended his oratorio *I Have a Dream* as a tribute to the late Martin Luther King. The libretto is based on statements by King, and includes Igbu[73] phrases that are chanted in the final section of Part 1. The work conveys the concerns of today's world, dramatized in a thirty-five minute musical journey focused on human dignity, love, hate, the tragedy of war, peace, beauty, poverty and a hope for genuine freedom.[74] This significant collaboration was a first and foreshadowed some of the more recent concerts programmed by the Cincinnati Symphony Orchestra and the May Festival. One intended outcome of the Civil Rights movement was integration. The undeniable results were finally felt in Cincinnati as members of diverse populations participated in arts projects and programs such as Furman's *I Have a Dream*.

At this time the Martin Luther King Coalition Chorale was formed with the intention of bringing black and white Cincinnatians together to sing. From segregated neighborhoods and from divergent creeds, people from different churches, synagogues, and mosques gathered in Avondale at Zion Baptist Church to counter King's notion that 11:00 Sunday morning was the most segregated hour in America. The singers who joined the King Chorale were indeed members of Cincinnati churches and choral groups and performed together at many black churches in the Tristate area. The group performed for the first time in January 1992 at Music Hall for the annual Martin Luther

King Day Memorial Program, directed by Dr. Catherine Roma and Bishop Todd O'Neal.

SOME DISTINGUISHED INDIVIDUALS

Loretta Catherine Cessor Manggrum (1896-1992), best known for her seven cantatas, learned piano at an early age from her mother. She was already playing piano at her church by age six, and later played piano for silent movies.

"Until the talkies came in. They had music for everything: a bird, a lion, happiness, walking along the street, murder. But by the time I could find the music, the picture was off the screen. So I made up my own music. I think that's where I began designing my own music."[75]

Manggrum performed to support her family while her husband completed pharmacy school. In 1945, at 49, she earned her diploma from Hughes High School. Between 1945 and 1951 she pursued summer studies at Fisk University in Nashville, Tennessee; Capital University in Columbus, Ohio; the Chicago Conservatory of Music; the Royal Conservatory in Toronto, Canada; and Marquette University in Milwaukee, Wisconsin. She received her Bachelor of Music degree in 1951 at age 55 from Ohio State University in Columbus.

Age was no deterrent to Manggrum. At 65 she began her teaching career in the Cincinnati Public Schools at Garfield School, where she taught for ten years. At 80 years of age, Manggrum began doctoral studies in composition at CCM, where she received an honorary doctorate in theory and composition in 1985 at the age of 88.

Manggrum's compositional style looks simple, but upon hearing it the listener realizes

that it is more complicated than it looks on paper. She incorporates fugal and contrapuntal techniques with fluidity, and her writing for voice is idiomatic. She moves easily between major, minor, modal, and chromatic harmonies. She served as choir director and organist at Union Baptist Church, Fosdic First Church of God, Brown Chapel AME, and finally Gaines United Methodist Church, where she was organist and choir director while she worked on her doctorate.

When Arthur Herndon discussed the talented musicians in Cincinnati's black churches, he mentioned, "Mrs. Manggrum wrote cantatas. She always envisioned doing [one] at the May Festival. She had not come on the scene for June Festival, but many Cincinnati church musicians sang *Behold* and *Watch*, her two great cantatas, at their churches."[76] In 2010 Eric V. Oliver started The Loretta Manggrum Chorale, not only to honor her name and her music, but to revive this strong interest in singing a wide range of choral music. The ensemble first performed *Behold* on December 12, 2010, and again in December 2011 at Bethel Baptist Church under the direction of Lillie Brown and Eric V. Oliver.

Arthur Herndon himself wanted to honor his role models, and in 1996 conducted a performance of Handel's *Messiah* with his Anna Howard Matthews Choir (named for the wife of Artie Matthews). Herndon had grown up in Cincinnati's West End and graduated from Hughes High School. It was his teacher, Helen Greer, who recognized his talent and

encouraged him to study music. At age 14, Herndon made his Cincinnati debut in the 1946 May Festival, singing Wren in Pierné's oratorio *St. Francis of Assisi*, with Eugene Goossens conducting. Because "the Conservatory was not admitting blacks to study," Herndon studied piano and violin privately, met Artie Matthews, and began studies at the Cosmopolitan School. "We fought very hard to break down that discrimination at the time, and were successful," he said.[77] By the time he was admitted as a vocal student to the newly merged College-Conservatory of Music, the climate had changed.

Arthur Herndon won a voice scholarship to Miami University, where he studied for two years before joining the United States Army. He served in the Korean War, and received an honorable discharge in 1956. After returning home, Herndon was determined to complete his music degree. He finished his Bachelor's degree in voice (1960), and later achieved a Master's degree in choral conducting (1981) from CCM. In 1960 he was named a John Hay Whitney Fellowship Scholar, and won a Fulbright grant to study in Italy. He apprenticed at the Rome Opera House under Luigi Ricci, one of the great Italian vocal coaches and a pupil of Puccini. He also studied at the Hochschule für Musik in Berlin. While in Europe, Herndon was invited by Thomas Schippers (conductor of the Cincinnati Symphony Orchestra from 1970 until his death in 1977) to sing at Italy's famous Spoleto Festival, where he was the featured tenor in Mendelssohn's *Elijah*, Strauss's *Der*

The May Festival Chorus, Christ Church Cathedral Choir and Westwood First Presbyterian Church Choir perform Henry Purcell's church anthem "O God, Thou Hast Cast Us Out," for chorus and organ, at the May Festival, May 7, 1958, Music Hall (Josef Krips, conductor). May Festival opened its doors to African American singers in 1956.

95

Rosenkavalier, and Rossini's *Stabat Mater*.

Because many American opera stages were closed to African Americans in the 1960s, Mr. Herndon pursued his singing career in Germany. He performed as the leading tenor at the Stadtstheater in Kassel, the first African American to do so. Returning to Ohio, Herndon joined the faculty of Central State University. During his tenure there, his choir was invited to perform in the Cincinnati May Festival's *Porgy and Bess,* conducted by James Levine, in 1976. Simon Estes sang the role of Porgy, Leona Mitchell sang Bess, and Florence Quivar was Serena. Cincinnati singer Clyde Williams performed Sportin' Life, and Lois Wilkins was Annie. The choir of Central State University was augmented by

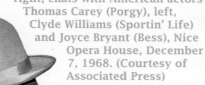

After a performance of George Gershwin's *Porgy and Bess*, Princess Grace of Monaco, right, chats with American actors Thomas Carey (Porgy), left, Clyde Williams (Sportin' Life) and Joyce Bryant (Bess), Nice Opera House, December 7, 1968. (Courtesy of Associated Press)

Cincinnati's African American

singers from area black churches, and Daphne Robinson suggests that their conductor, Arthur Herndon, may well have been responsible for the inclusion of local artists Lois Wilkins and Clyde Williams in the cast. His niece remarked, "He saw good in everyone and could pull greatness out of anybody."[78]

Arthur Herndon served as minister of music at Allen Temple AME in Bond Hill and Calvary United Methodist Church in Evanston. One of his goals was to keep the classical choral tradition alive in the African American church community. His church choir, the Anna Howard Matthews Choir, had been founded by Anna Howard in 1900 and had a long reputation as an outstanding ensemble. He decided to perform Handel's *Messiah* as a tribute to black church and choral musicians, and named Artie Matthews, Richard Bush, Newell Fitzpatrick, Jefferson Henderson, Loretta Manggrum, Bryne Camp, Eloise Clark, Coleman Conway, Geneva Craig, William T. Gee, Clinton Gibbs, Helen Greer, Tommie Harris, Charles F. Keys, James V. Roach, Noah W. Ryder, Helen Saunders, Clyde Williams, Andrew Johnson, Russell Lamont, John Quartes, and Harold D. Smith.

Lillie Harrison Brown, a native Cincinnatian and contemporary of Arthur Herndon, graduated from the College-Conservatory of Music in 1961. For over thirty years, she has served as music director of Bethel Baptist Church. Ms. Brown is frequently sought out when area arts organizations want participation from talented singers in the African American community. Several times, Lillie Brown coached and prepared her own church choir and other area church choristers in collaborations on projects with Carmon DeLeone and the Cincinnati Ballet, including outdoor mini-festivals during the 1980s and the ballet *With Timbrel and Dance, Praise His Name*.[79]

Daphne Robinson has insisted, "Cincinnati area black church musicians have been a part of the musical fabric and education of many African American citizens. Hence it is important that their achievements and contributions to Cincinnati's cultural life be recognized. There has always been a concentration of trained church musicians who teach classical music, anthems, hymns, and spirituals, as well as traditional and contemporary gospel music."[80]

THE AMERICAN NEGRO SPIRITUAL FESTIVAL

In 1981, the American Negro Spiritual Festival (ANSF) was established in Cincinnati in order to raise funds for the Human Involvement Project (HIP) when cuts in the city's human services budget threatened to close this vital organization. HIP served at-risk youth and their families in inner-city Cincinnati. Althea Day, executive director of the ANSF, said she had several goals in mind: "To preserve the spiritual as a musical art form and increase awareness as to what it is," and "to help various college choirs preserve the Negro Spiritual." She spelled out the mission even more clearly when she continued:

"Spirituals are unique. They were sung and used for a special purpose. These circumstances no longer exist, but the influence is immense. Spirituals are the basis for gospel, blues, jazz, and rock and roll. They all have a certain theme that goes back to the source. Spirituals always have a sense of hope, even in the saddest songs that came out of the worst situations. It's a force that transcends lines of race, gender, and class. How else can you explain why spirituals are so beloved all over the world by so many different people?"[81]

Every March in Cincinnati from 1982 to 1998, college and university choirs came to Music Hall to compete for the top prize of $5,000. The festival was designed to work in four-year cycles. Four choirs would compete each year; during the fifth year the winners from the previous four years would compete against each other. Performance requirements and standards were determined by an eighteen-member committee made up of local conductors and musicians. Each choir had to perform three spirituals from a list of more than 65, including one required piece. All selections were to be performed *a cappella* and choruses were rated on a 100-point system based on such factors as phonation, style, articulation, and pitch. Well known musicians and artists served as honorary chairpersons for the festival, among them Odetta, Nikki Giovanni, Jennifer Holliday, and William Warfield. Members of the Competition Criteria Committee, who served for the duration of the ANSF concerts, included such local school and church musicians as Lillian Brown, Jacqueline Carr, Carolyn Mitchell, Ruth Phillips, Daphne W. Robinson, Irma Tillery, and Ada Walton. Other area musicians included Eric V. Oliver, Sherrie Turner, and Josephine Justice.[82]

Many of the competing choirs came from predominantly black colleges and universities

Pictures from left to right: Althea Day, founder American Negro Spiritual Festival. Lillian Brown, prominent director in the Cincinnati area, with Cincinnati Ballet and local churches. Ruth Phillips, long-time director of choral activities at Union Baptist Church. Daphne Robinson, director of music at Hartwell United Methodist Church, Irma Tillery, music director and organist at St. Andrews Episcopal Church, Sherrie Turner, director of music, St. Peter's United Church of Christ.

THE HUMAN INVOLVEMENT PROJECT'S
(A United Appeal Agency)

TENTH ANNUAL
AMERICAN NEGRO
SPIRITUAL FESTIVAL

from across the south and Midwest, but groups from other institutions also competed: for example, singers from Morgan State University (Baltimore, Maryland); a choir of students from Butler University of Indianapolis; the Black Student Union Choir from Denison University (Ohio); The Meistersingers, a choir from Tennessee State at Nashville; choristers from North Carolina A&T (Greensboro, NC), and Knoxville (Tennessee) College; the Concert Choir from Kentucky State University at Frankfort; choruses of Central State University and Wilberforce University (Ohio); the University Choir from Xavier University of Louisiana; singers from Philander Smith College of Little Rock, Arkansas, Rust College (Holly Springs, Mississippi), and many more. Occasionally the four competing choirs sang together, as in 1984 when all 134 voices performed "A New Song," a spiritual written by Cincinnati composer Loretta Manggrum.

In 1991, for the tenth anniversary of the ANSF, Althea Day added a new ingredient. She widened the circle of influence to include elementary school choirs. Four groups competed for monetary prizes in the second year: Hamilton's Harrison Elementary School, and three Cincinnati schools: Hoffman, Pleasant Hill, and Silverton. The ANSF Youth Festivals continued until 1998. By 1993, the winning school choir was performing with the college choirs at Music Hall before the competition began.

Althea Day observed, "Back in the 1960s and 1970s choirs stopped performing spirituals and people weren't interested in listening, especially to *a cappella* singing."[83] Through her ingenious efforts to provide ongoing to support

for the Human Involvement Project, Day created a legacy for the city of Cincinnati. The festival was tied to HIP's mission to work with youth, especially those struggling to survive, and promoted interest and inspired people of all ages to understand the true meaning of the spirituals and their relevance to today's issues.

Althea Day also was the "prime mover for another project that involved a large volunteer chorus and dramatic artists. Day served as director and producer for *River Crossing,* a production that opened with a reenactment of a slave family crossing the Ohio River. Through drama and singing, it told the story of how African American communities developed in settlements such as Cincinnati's Bucktown and Little Africa, how they developed churches, and how they founded schools for colored children.[84]

DEVELOPMENTS OF THE 1990s

In the early 1990s, Clinton J. Bean (Minister of Music at Zion Baptist) and Eric V. Oliver (Minister of Music at Mt. Zion Baptist) created a city-wide workshop to "provide participants with information, diverse music and musical techniques which can be shared with Greater Cincinnati area choirs." Guest clinician Dr. Margaret Pleasant Douroux traveled to Cincinnati from Los Angeles to lead the workshop and to present her compositions. Participating singers performed hymns, anthems and spirituals, as well as traditional and contemporary gospel.[85]

William Caldwell, director of Vocal and Choral Activities since 1979 at Central State University, Ohio's only historically black

Top: Jackson State University Chorale, 16th American Negro Spiritual Festival, 1997.
Bottom: Rust College *a cappella* choir, 15th ANSF, 1996, Music Hall, Zebedee Jones, director. (Courtesy of *Cincinnati Enquirer*)

The highly acclaimed Central
State University Chorus, under
the direction of William Caldwell
since 1979, sings choral music of
all periods and styles, including
the black spiritual. In 1993, the Chorus
performed with Erich Kunzel and the
Cincinnati Pops Orchestra, and has recorded
two Telarc CDs with the CPO. Recent tours have
included Germany and Italy. Plans are underway
for performances in China in 2012.

The MLK Chorale, founded in 1991, features talented local solo artists. Pictured here: John Wesley Wright and Linda O'Neal. (Courtesy of Roy Goosbey) The Chorale brings together men and women from area churches and choral ensembles who sing for the annual city-wide King Celebration each January.

public university, has played an important role in choral music in both Dayton and Cincinnati. He has appeared widely as a baritone soloist, and his work providing well-prepared choruses has won praise and invitations to work with the Cincinnati Pops, the May Festival, and the Dayton Philharmonic. In February 1993 the chorus of Central State was a major player in *A Gospel Celebration*, with Erich Kunzel and the Pops, performing traditional spirituals and gospel arrangements. They shared the stage with the Chorus of Azusa Pacific University and Cab Calloway. In 2002, conductor James Conlon and the May Festival invited the Central State University Chorus to perform "His Eye Is on the Sparrow," and "Jesus Is a Rock in a Weary Land," arrangements for chorus and orchestra by Dayton Philharmonic's Neal Gittleman.

In 1999, a major production called *A Mighty Spirit* was presented at Cincinnati's Aronoff Center for the Arts. Sherrie Turner was Artistic Director and responsible for the coordination of the musical masses. Choral organizations included the Baroque Choral Ensemble, Kentucky State University's Concert Choir, the Cincinnati Boychoir, the Children's Choir of Cincinnati's School for Creative and Performing Arts, the Voices of Bethel, the Peace Baptist Church Choir,

Pictures on the next pages, top: *A Mighty Spirit*, directed by Sherrie Turner. Bottom: Lois Shegog directs MLK Chorale with Cincinnati Public School students. Top: Eric V. Oliver, Minister of Music at Zion Baptist Church. Bottom: Everette Moore conducts at Zion Baptist Church.

and additional volunteer singers from the Cincinnati area. Other notable participants were the Dayton Contemporary Dance Company and O'Ginga Kamisi and his African Drum and Dance Ensemble.

In 2001 the Cincinnati Symphony Orchestra (CSO), through its commitment to a diversity and inclusion program, initiated *Classical Roots: Linking Cultures through Music*. The CSO and four partner churches, Lincoln Heights Missionary Baptist, Quinn Chapel AME, Zion Baptist, and Allen Temple AME, "sought to link cultures through music and to cultivate an appreciation for diversity." *Classical Roots: Spirituals Heights*, the first program, presented members of the CSO, with guest artist William Henry Caldwell singing arrangements by Harry T. Burleigh and songs by Stephen Foster. Each year, chamber-size instrumental groups performed at different churches. By 2006, a children's choir was added, and the "Ballad of the Underground Railroad" by Rene Boyer was performed. Sherrie Turner and Geneva Woode prepared the children's choir for conductor John Morris Russell. In 2007, the St. Peter's United Church of Christ Community Chorale joined the above-mentioned choirs, and their director, Sherrie Turner, led the combined choirs in Moses Hogan's "Hear My Prayer."

In March 2011, *Classical Roots* moved to Music Hall, where the program *Lift Ev'ry Voice* featured internationally acclaimed artists as well as local talent, including conductor Michael Morgan, soprano Angela Brown, and tenor Rodrick Dixon. Without doubt, the most stunning part of the evening was the 150-voice Community Mass Choir composed of singers from local, predominantly black churches, who sang traditional and modern spirituals and classical choral works. Some of the most highly regarded church ministers of music in the area, among them Dr. Robert Gazaway (Allen Temple AME); Rev. Darryl Cherry (Lincoln Heights Missionary Baptist Church); Eric V. Oliver (Zion Baptist Church); and Geneva Kinard Woode (Quinn Chapel AME Church), prepared the choir and accompanied some of the pieces that were performed: works by Ingrid Woode and the Reverend Darryl Cherry, and arrangements of traditional spirituals by Julie Spangler and Eric V. Oliver. The program opened with J. Rosamond and James Weldon Johnson's "Lift Ev'ry Voice," sung by both choir and audience, and the final number, "The Hallelujah Chorus" from *Too Hot to Handel,* brought audience members to their feet in ovation after ovation.[86]

The Martin Luther King Chorale was started when two industrious members

of MUSE, Cincinnati's Women's Choir, joined the Martin Luther King Jr. Coalition and volunteered to create an interracial, interdenominational choir to perform at the annual King Day Memorial Program celebrating the life and legacy of Dr. Martin Luther King, Jr. In 1991 Dr. Catherine Roma and Gilda Turner went to area churches to recruit singers for the Chorale. In its first year (January 1992), the choir consisted of approximately 60 voices and performed movements from *Requiem for Brother Martin*, by Reverend Charles Walker of Nineteenth Street Baptist Church in Philadelphia, and "My Lord What a Morning," by H.T. Burleigh. Since then, Bishop Todd O'Neal (House of Joy Christian Ministries) and Dr. Catherine Roma (St. John's Unitarian Universalist Church) have co-directed the chorus, which has swelled to over 120 voices.

The mission of the King Chorale matches that of the King Coalition. It intentionally brings together people of diverse religious backgrounds (Catholic, Baha'i, Methodist, Presbyterian, Episcopal, Lutheran, Unitarian, Hindu, Jewish, Quaker, Muslim, Pentecostal, and Earth-based faiths), along with unchurched people from city and suburban neighborhoods, to sing together, to connect to each other through musical relationships, and to uphold and manifest the principles of King's dream. The group has performed larger works: *Free at Last: A Portrait of Martin Luther King, Jr.,* by Lena McLin; *His Light Still Shines*, by Moses Hogan; *Requiem for Brother Martin*, by Reverend Charles Walker, classic Negro spirituals arranged by William Dawson, Hall Johnson, Moses Hogan, Undine Smith Moore, Andre Thomas, Rosephanye Powell, and

on, 1824 – 2012

The Classical Roots concert in 2011 featured singers from area church choirs and the Cincinnati Symphony Orchestra. This was the tenth anniversary of the CSO's successful Classical Roots: Linking Cultures through Music project.

211

Pictures from left to right: Voices of Freedom Chorus at the ground breaking for the National Underground Railroad Freedom Center, June 2002. (Courtesy of Melvin Grier) Singers from the King Chorale, January 2012. (Courtesy of Philip Groshong) Singers at Allen Temple, *Opera Goes to Church!* performance, Summer 2011. The Voices of Freedom Chorus at the ground breaking of the National Underground Railroad Freedom Center. (Courtesy of *Cincinnati Enquirer*)

jazz, and classical music, was created to bring people together through the power of choral music and opera at many diverse religious centers throughout the Greater Cincinnati area. Since 2006, Cincinnati Opera has partnered with Allen Temple A.M.E Church in Bond Hill, St. Barnabas Episcopal Church in Montgomery, Christo Rey Catholic Parish in Erlanger, Kentucky, and College Hill Presbyterian Church in College Hill. The programs feature internationally renowned opera stars from Cincinnati Opera's main stage summer season with choristers from some of Cincinnati's most outstanding church choirs. The 2011 season of *Opera Goes to Church*! fostered some very special connections throughout the Greater Cincinnati community, including the creation and performance of the College Hill Community Choir, a group comprised of participants from fourteen religious institutions of various denominations, ages,[87] races, ethnicities, and physical capabilities.[88]

Opera Goes to Church! was an outgrowth of community programming supporting Cincinnati Opera's first major commission, *Margaret Garner*. A co-commission with Michigan Opera Theatre and Opera Company of Philadelphia, *Margaret Garner* premiered in Cincinnati in 2005 to commemorate the opening of the National Underground Railroad Freedom Center. This opera, set in 1857, highlights the true story of a woman enslaved in Boone County, Kentucky and featured a local thirty-voice African American chorus—an additional first for Cincinnati Opera. Composer Richard Danielpour notes:

"More than anything else, *Margaret Garner* is an opera that reminds us that we all belong to the same human family, and it demonstrates what can happen when we forget this fundamental

Pictures from left to right: Dr. Robert Gazaway, Minister of Music at Allen Temple AME, leads singers at *Opera Goes to Church!*, Bond Hill. The Cincinnati Opera's co-commission, *Margaret Garner*, libretto by Toni Morrison. Combined singers from College Hill churches for *Opera Goes to Church!*, College Hill Presbyterian Church. (Courtesy of Philip Groshong)

truth. While slavery has been outlawed in the United States since 1865, its lingering effects have proven over the years that the issues in our country concerning race, class, and the true meaning of freedom are in no way resolved. Visiting Washington, D.C. today, one can see memorials to heroes from every war and cause, but there is not one memorial to the people who suffered under the institution of slavery. It is my hope that *Margaret Garner* will both memorialize and remind us of what we as a society are so easily inclined to forget."[89]

In order to continue to demonstrate the company's commitment to diversity, in 2007 Cincinnati Opera commissioned composer Adolphus Hailstork to write an opera about the life of abolitionist and Underground Railroad conductor John P. Parker. The family opera *Rise for Freedom: The John P. Parker Story* featured a twenty-two person cast, including nine principal roles for African Americans. Adolphus Hailstork also composed "Earthrise," a work for double chorus and orchestra commissioned by the May Festival in 2006 to promote healing following the 2000 riots. The piece featured a white chorus on one side of the risers and an African American chorus on the other side, who by the end form a visual metaphor by interweaving to create a racially harmonic gesture.

On the musical soundtrack to Cincinnati's new day, many voices resonate. Throughout the city, there are echoes of our singing forebears in the African American musical tradition. Music continues to reign in countless churches, community buildings, public and private schools, and open-air festivals. The rich history of black music in the Queen City continues to assert its voice and its place in both the classical canon (witness the opera *Margaret Garner)* and the colloquial commons (for example, at the annual Midwest Black Family Reunion each August). Continued attention to this enduring, inspiring art form will only increase its potency and its place in America's musical narrative.

In 2007, the Cincinnati Opera Co. commissioned Adolphus Hailstork to write *Rise for Freedom: The John P. Parker Story*, about the life of abolitionist and Underground Railroad conductor John P. Parker. (Courtesy of Philip Groshong)

NOTES

1. George Cary, "The Colored American," August 10, 1838.

2. Wendell P. Dabney, *Cincinnati's Colored Citizens: Historical, Sociological and Biographical* (Cincinnati: The Dabney Publishing Company, 1926) and Lyle Koehler, *Cincinnati's Black People: A Chronology and Bibliography, 1787-1982* (Cincinnati: Lyle Koehler, 1986).

3. Nikki M. Taylor, *Frontiers of Freedom: Cincinnati's Black Community 1802-1868* (Athens, OH: Ohio University Press, 2005), 2.

4. Ibid., 3-4.

5. Koehler, *Cincinnati's Black People*, 2-4

6. Taylor, *Frontiers of Freedom*, 24.

7. Ibid., 25.

8. Ibid., 151.

9. Eileen Southern, *The Music of Black Americans: A History*, 3rd edition (New York: W. W. Norton, 1997), 52.

10. Robert Gazaway, interview with author, August, 23, 2011.

11. Eric V. Oliver, interview with author, September 20, 2011.

12. Wilbur A Page, *History of Union Baptist Church* (Cincinnati: Selby Service/Roxy Press), 11.

13. A melodeon is a type of nineteenth-century reed organ with foot-operated vacuum bellows and a piano keyboard.

14. *The Christian Recorder*, September 24, 1864, 1

15. *The Christian Recorder*, September 23, 1865, 2

16. Dena J. Epstein, *Sinful Tunes and Spirituals: Black Folk Music to the Civil War* (Urbana, IL: University of Illinois Press, 1977), 223.

17. George Leonard White (1838-1895), a white man, had moved to Ohio at the age of 20. While not a singer himself, he developed a talent for interpreting music and began directing choirs at various schools and churches in Ohio, where he also founded a black Sunday school.

18. Ella Sheppard (Moore) had been born into slavery. Her father purchased her freedom at the age of three, and they moved to Cincinnati in 1857. He bought Ella a piano, sent her to the Seventh Street Colored School, and arranged for her to take music lessons. In Cincinnati, Sheppard took voice lessons with a prominent white teacher who recognized her talent and agreed to teach her, but only on the condition than Ella enter her home through the back door and come only at night. "Ella Sheppard, Soprano," *Jubilee Singers: Sacrifice and Glory*, http://www.pbs.org/wgbh/amex/singers/, accessed September 1, 2011

19. G. D. Pike, *Jubilee Singers and Their Campaign for Twenty Thousand Dollars* (Boston: Lee and Shepard Publishers, 1873), 75.

20. Ibid., 76.

21. Mozart Hall opened in 1863, and in 1874 was converted as the Grand Opera House seating 3,000.

22. David S. Reynolds, *Mightier than the Sword, Uncle Tom's Cabin and the Battle for America* (New York: W. W. Norton and Co. Inc, 2012), 181.

23. Toni P. Anderson, T*ell Them We Are Singing for Jesus: The Original Fisk Jubilee Singers and Christian Reconstruction, 1871-1878* (Macon, GA: Mercer University Press, 2010), 50.

24. *Esther the Beautiful Queen*, by W. B. Bradley, is the story of the Jews in Babylon, as told in music. The work became well established in the repertoire of community choruses.

25. Under the pseudonym Aristides, Williams wrote for the *Cincinnati Commercial* for two years (1876-78).

26. Aristides, "The 'Cantata of Esther' by the Choral Society—Music Among the Colored People," *Cincinnati Commercial*, May 19, 1878, 4.

27. Ibid.

28. John Hope Franklin, *George Washington Williams: A Biography* (Chicago: University of Chicago Press, 1985), 41.

29. Peter H. Clark, after whom Clark Montessori School is named, graduated from Gilmore High School.

30. Taylor, *Frontiers of Freedom*, 162.

31. Dabney, *Cincinnati's Colored Citizens*, 177.

32. Frederick Douglass Papers, August 31, 1855, held at the Library of Congress.

33. Ibid.

34. *The Christian Recorder*, January 31, 1863, 18

35. Steven C. Tracy, *Going to Cincinnati: A History of the Blues in the Queen City* (Urbana: University of Illinois Press, 1993), xxi.

36. In *Ragtime: Its History, Composers, and Music* (New York: Schirmer Books, 1985, 86), John Edward Hasse observes: "It is ironic and tragic that the rejection of ragtime by proper musical circles as sinful and immoral music—indeed the segregation for decades of black musics from the established white culture—could have caused a gifted man like Matthews to turn his back on ragtime."

37. *International Dictionary of Black Composers*, s.v. "Artie Matthews."

38. *Cincinnati Post Times-Star*, March 27, 1958, 6.

39. "Institution Is Tribute to Man's Drive: Cosmopolitan School of Music Now Is Flourishing," *Cincinnati Post*, April 6, 1943, 22:5.

40. M. Ruth Brown Phillips, interview with the author, Thursday, August 25, 2011.

41. Andrea Tuttle Kornbluh, "Municipal Harmony: Cultural Pluralism, Public Recreation, and Race Relations," in *Historical Roots of the Urban Crisis: African Americans in the Industrial City*, ed. Henry Louis Taylor and Walter Hill (New York: Garland Publishing Co., 2000), 83.

42. *Annual Report of the Public Recreation Commission* (Cincinnati 1930),

43. Ibid.

44. J. Wesley Jones was active in Chicago as a church organist and choir director.

45. *Annual Report of the Public Recreation Commission* (Cincinnati, 1933), 40

46. "The Community Music Program in Cincinnati," by Harry F. Glore, p. 259 and http://www.archive.org/details/yearbookogthemus01058mbp, accessed September 3, 2011

47. Ibid., 261.

48. *Annual Report of the Public Recreation Commission* (Cincinnati, 1935), 46.

49. Daphne Robinson, e-mail to author, August 23, 2011.

50. Lyle Koehler, *Cincinnati's Black People*, 159.

51. Ibid., 161.

52. *Annual Report of the Public Recreation Commission* (Cincinnati, 1939), 41.

53. *The New Grove Dictionary of Music and Musicians*, s.v "Clarence Cameron White."

54. *Cincinnati Enquirer*, February 22, 1940

55. *Cincinnati Post*, April 10, 1939.

56. Ibid.

57. *Cincinnati Times-Star*, June 12, 1948, 6.

58. Janelle Gelfand, obituary of Estella Rowe, *Cincinnati Enquirer*, June 2, 2000.

59. *Cincinnati Times-Star*, June 11, 1951, 14:6.

60. Janelle Gelfand, unpublished interview with Arthur Herndon, 2005.

61. Program booklet for *50th Anniversary Concert*, Sunday, July 19, 1992, from Ann Greene's collection.

62. Ibid.

63. Clyde Williams, a graduate of the College-Conservatory of Music, went on to New York as a professional singer and dancer. In 1976 he returned to Cincinnati to perform the role of Sportin' Life in the May Festival's concert presentation of *Porgy and Bess*.

64. Daphne Robinson, "The Diversity of African American Cultural Expression" (unpublished article, Cincinnati 2011).

65. John Bailey, interview with the author, Monday, July 25, 2011.

66. Ibid.

67. Printed information from Ann Greene collection.

68. Ann Greene, author interview, June 23, 2011.

69. Ibid.

70. Ibid.

71. Correspondence from Betty J. Smith to Greta Gibson, former members of BCE, August 10, 2011.

72. Ann Greene, interview with author, Tuesday, June 23, 2011.

73. Spelled in various ways, Igbu, Igbo, or Ibu is a native language of the Igbo people, an ethnic group located primarily in southeastern Nigeria.

74. Furman, in *Cincinnati Symphony Orchestra* Program, January 22-23, 1971.

75. Patricia Mroczek, "Loretta Manggrum: A Woman and Her Music," *Sonneck Society for American Music Bulletin* 14, no. 2 (1988): 55-57.

76. Gelfand, unpublished interview with Arthur Herndon.

77. Ibid.

78. Robinson, "The Diversity of African American Cultural Expression."

79. Ibid.

80. Ibid

81. *Cincinnati Enquirer*, March 15, 1984, D15:1, and March 23, 1987, 1b:2.

82. Robinson, "The Diversity of African American Cultural Expression."

83. *Cincinnati Post*, March 21, 1996, 1b+Pic.

84. Robinson, "The Diversity of African American Cultural Expression."

85. Materials provided by Eric V. Oliver.

86. The work captures the essential core of Handel's *Messiah* and reinterprets it with the rhythms and the harmonic language of R&B, jazz, and gospel.

87. Publicity from *Opera Goes to Church!* provided by Tracy L. Wilson. *Opera Goes to Church!* was created by Cincinnati Opera's Director of Community Relations, Tracy L. Wilson.

88. Ibid.

89. "*Margaret Garner*, Richard Danielpour." Schirmer, http://schirmer.com (accessed November 16, 2011).

BIBLIOGRAPHY

Anderson, Toni P. *"Tell Them We Are Singing for Jesus." The Original Fisk Jubilee Singers and Christian Reconstruction, 1871-1878.* Macon: Mercer University Press, 2010.

Austerlitz, Emanuel. *Cincinnati from 1800 to 1875: A Condensed History of Cincinnati Combined with Exposition Guide for 1875. Fully Illustrated, Together with a Description of Pictures and Works of Art, Exhibited at the Cincinnati Industrial Exposition, 1875.* Cincinnati: Bloch & Co., [1875].

Board, Helen. *Bertha Baur: A Woman of Note.* Philadelphia: Dorrance and Company, 1971.

Boehle, Rose Angela, O.S.U. *Maria Longworth: A Biography.* Dayton: Landfall Press, 1990.

Brasch, Irving. "History of Secondary Education in the Parochial Schools of Hamilton County, Ohio." MEd thesis, University of Cincinnati, 1938.

Burgheim, Max. *Cincinnati in Wort und Bild: Nach authentischen Quellen bearbeitet und zusammengestellt.* Cincinnati: n. p., 1888.

Chambrun, Clara Longworth, Comtesse de. *Cincinnati: Story of the Queen City.* New York: C. Scribner's Sons, 1939.

"Charles Aiken." In *Golden Jubilee Souvenir, 1878-1928.* Cincinnati: Cincinnati Music Hall Association, 1928, 73-77.

Chorus Music of the May Festival, 1873. Cincinnati: [John Church], 1873.

"Cincinnati Independent Colored School System." Columbus: Ohio Historical Society, 2010. *http://www.ohiohistorycentral. org/entry.php?rec=856* , accessed June 7, 2010.

Cincinnati Sings—A Choral History 1788-1988. Cincinnati: Cincinnati Musical Festival Association, 1988.

The Cincinnati Symphony Orchestra: Centennial Portraits. Cincinnati: Cincinnati Symphony Orchestra, 1994.

Cincinnati und sein Deutschthum. Cincinnati: Queen City, 1901.

The Cincinnatian. Cincinnati: Students of the University of Cincinnati, 1894- .

Dabney, W. P. *Cincinnati's Colored Citizens.* Cincinnati: Dabney Publishing Company, 1926.

Doolin, Craig A. "Festival by Committee: The Planning and Performances of the First Cincinnati May Festival of 1873." MA thesis, Marshall University, 1997.

"The Early History of Cincinnati Public Schools." *http://www.cpsboe.k12.oh.us/general/History/History.html*, accessed June 10, 2010.

Ebertz, Mary Joline, R.S.M. "A History of the Development of Music Education in the Archdiocese of Cincinnati." EdD dissertation, University of Cincinnati, 1955.

Epstein, Dena. *Sinful Tunes and Spirituals: Black Folk Music to the Civil War.* Urbana: University of Illinois Press, 1977.

The Fine Arts Guide to Ohio, Season 1929-30. Fine Arts Service of Ohio, compiler. Cleveland and Cincinnati: Fine Arts Service, 1929.

Foreman, B. J. *The College-Conservatory of Music 1867-1992: CCM 125,* ed. Jerri Roberts. [Cincinnati:] University of Cincinnati, [1992].

Fortin, Roger A. *To See Great Wonders: A History of Xavier University 1831-2006.* Scranton, PA: University of Scranton Press, 2006.

Frank, Leonie. *Musical Life in Early Cincinnati and the Origin of the May Festival.* Cincinnati: Ruter Press, 1932.

Franklin, John Hope. *George Washington Williams: A Biography.* Chicago: University of Chicago Press, 1985.

Gary, Charles L. "A History of Music Education in the Cincinnati Public Schools." EdD dissertation, University of Cincinnati, 1951.

Genovese, Eugene D. *Roll, Jordan, Roll: The World the Slaves Made.* New York: Vintage Books, 1972.

Giglierano, Geoffrey J., and Deborah A. Overmyer, with Frederic L. Propas. *The Bicentennial Guide to Greater Cincinnati.* Cincinnati: Cincinnati Historical Society, 1988.

Golden Jubilee Saengerfest: Cincinnati 1899. Cincinnati: n. p., 1899.

Goss, Charles Frederic. *Cincinnati, the Queen City.* 4 vols. Chicago and Cincinnati: S. J. Clarke Publishing Co., 1912.

Grace, Kevin, and Greg Hand. *The University of Cincinnati.* Montgomery, AL: Community Communications, 1995.

Greve, Charles Theodore. *Centennial History of Cincinnati and Representative Citizens.* 2 vols. Chicago: Biographical Publishing Company, 1904.

Hasse, John Edward. *Ragtime: Its History, Composers, and Music.* New York: Schirmer Books, 1985.

Hebble, Charles R., and Frank P. Goodwin. *The Citizens Book.* Cincinnati: Stewart, 1916.

Howe, Granville L., and William Smythe Matthews Babcock. *A Hundred Years of Music in America.* Chicago: Howe, 1900.

Hurley, Daniel. *Cincinnati, the Queen City.* Cincinnati: Cincinnati Historical Society, 1982.

Jasen, David A. *Rags and Ragtime: A Musical History.* New York: The Seabury Press, 1978.

Koehler, Lyle. *Cincinnati's Black People: A Chronology and Bibliography, 1787-1982.* Cincinnati: Cincinnati Arts Consortium, 1986.

Kornbluh, Andrea T. "Municipal Harmony: Cultural Pluralism, Public Recreation, and Race Relations." In *Historical Roots of the Urban Crisis: African Americans in the Industrial City, 1900-1950,* ed. Henry Louis Taylor, Jr. New York: Garland, 2000.

Lewis, John. "An Historical Study of the Origin and Development of the Cincinnati Conservatory of Music." EdD dissertation, University of Cincinnati, 1943.

Lovell, Jr., John. *Black Song: The Forge and the Flame. The Story of How the Afro-American Spiritual Was Hammered Out*. New York: Paragon House, 1972.

Luening, Eugene. "The Art of Singing and Music in America." In *Milwaukee: A Guide to the Cream City, for Visitors and Citizens. Giving a History of the Settlement, Development and Present Importance of the City, with a Chronology of Interesting Events: A Souvenir of the 24th Saengerfest of the N[orth] A[merican] Saengerbund*. Milwaukee: Caspar & Zahn, 1886.

Mees, Arthur. *Choirs and Choral Music*. London: John Murray, 1901.

Moore, Gina Ruffin. *Black America Series: Cincinnati*. Charleston, SC: Arcadia, 2009.

Nicholes, Walter M. "The Educational Development of Blacks in Cincinnati from 1800 to the Present." EdD dissertation, University of Cincinnati, 1977.

Nord-Amerikanischer Saengerbund. http://www.nasaengerbund.org.

Ohio Division of Elementary and Secondary Education. "The Musical Heritage of Ohio." N.p.: Typescript, n.d.

Orlando, Vincent A. "An Historical Study of the Origin and Development of the College of Music of Cincinnati." EdD dissertation, University of Cincinnati, 1946.

Osborne, William. *Music in Ohio*. Kent, OH, and London: Kent State University Press, 2004.

Peltz, Carl. "Historical Sketch of the North American Saengerbund." In *Andenken an das Goldene Jubilaeum des Nordamerikanischen Saengerbundes*. Cincinnati: Nord-Amerikanischer Sängerbund, 1899.

Pike, G. D. *Jubilee Singers and Their Campaign for Twenty Thousand Dollars*. Boston: Lee and Shepard, 1873.

Reynolds, David S. *Mightier Than the Sword: Uncle Tom's Cabin and the Battle for America*. New York: W. W. Norton & Co., 2012.

Sammons, Jeffrey T. *Beyond the Ring: The Role of Boxing in American Society*. Urbana: University of Illinois Press, 1990.

Second Vatican Council. http://mb-soft.com/believe/txs/secondvc.htm, accessed August 25, 2010.

II Vatican Council—A Fulltext Search Engine of All Documents http://stjosef.at/council/search/search/, accessed August 25, 2010.

Sheblessy, Sylvia Kleve. *100 Years of the Cincinnati May Festival*. Cincinnati: privately printed, 1973.

Shotwell, John. *A History of the Schools of Cincinnati*. Cincinnati: School Life Co., 1902.

Soriano, Constantine F. "Cincinnati Music Readers." MM thesis, University of Cincinnati, 1957.

Souder, Mary Jo. "The College-Conservatory of Music of Cincinnati 1955-1962: A History." MM thesis, University of Cincinnati, 1970.

Southern, Eileen. *The Music of Black Americans: A History*. 3rd ed. New York: W. W. Norton & Co., 1997.

_____. *Readings in Black American Music*. 2nd ed. New York: W. W. Norton & Co., 1983.

Spanhaimer, Sr. Mary Edmund. "Heinrich Ammin Ratterman: German-American Author, Poet, and Historian, 1832-1923." PhD dissertation, Catholic University of America, 1937.

Thierstein, Eldred A. *Cincinnati Opera: From the Zoo to Music Hall*. Hillsdale, MI: Deerstone Books, 1995.

Thomas, Regina Coleman. "Historical Development of the Negro Elementary Schools of Cincinnati, Ohio." MEd thesis, University of Cincinnati, 1944.

Thompson, Jewel Taylor. *Samuel Coleridge Taylor: The Development of His Compositional Style*. Metuchen, NJ: Scarecrow Press, 1994.

Tolzmann, Don Heinrich. *Cincinnati's German Heritage*. Bowie, MD: Heritage, 1994.

_____. *The German-American Experience*. Amherst, NY: Humanity Books, 2000.

_____. *German Americana: Selected Essays*. Milford, OH: Little Miami, 2009.

_____. *German Cincinnati*. Charleston, SC: Arcadia, 2005.

_____. *German Heritage Guide to the Greater Cincinnati Area*. 2nd ed. Milford, OH: Little Miami, 2007.

_____. *The Cincinnati Germans after the Great War*. New York: Lang, 1987.

_____. "The Survival of an Ethnic Community: The Cincinnati Germans, 1918 through 1932." PhD dissertation, University of Cincinnati, 1983.

Tracy, Steven C. *Going to Cincinnati: A History of the Blues in the Queen City*. Urbana: University of Illinois Press, 1993.

Tunison, F[rank] E. *Presto! From the Singing School to the May Musical Festival*. Cincinnati: E. H. Beasley, 1888.

Travis, Lucinda Katheryne. "A Study of Vocal Programs at the Cincinnati Conservatory of Music 1930-1950." MM thesis, Cincinnati Conservatory of Music, 1950.

Wolz, Larry. "The College of Music of Cincinnati: A Centennial Tribute." *Bulletin of the Cincinnati Historical Society* 36 #2 (1978): 104-115.

_____. "Opera in Cincinnati: The Years before the Zoo, 1801-1920." PhD dissertation, University of Cincinnati, 1983.

ABOUT THE AUTHORS

Craig Doolin has been involved in nearly every aspect of music making and research over the past 40 years. He has been a band director, composer, arranger, and radio host. As a clarinetist and woodwind specialist, he has performed throughout the Ohio Valley. As a musicologist, he has written extensively about concert repertoire. Craig is the owner of Orpheus Music Prose, a successful program notes company that supplies writings to orchestras across North America. While still a master's student, he wrote the first full-length history of the first Cincinnati May Festival. Future projects include a musicology podcast and research on popular music of the 1960s. Craig lives in Norwood, Ohio, with his partner, James Dreigon, and their Boston terrier, Cosmo.

Karin Pendle has been involved in choral music since the age of eight, when she joined the children's choir at her Minneapolis church. Since then she has performed in choruses with the Minnesota Orchestra, the Cleveland Orchestra, the London (Ontario) Symphony, and the Cincinnati Symphony, where she also sang small solos in the May Festival. She holds a PhD in musicology from the University of Illinois and has taught at Oberlin College, the University of Western Ontario, and the College-Conservatory of Music at the University of Cincinnati. Her publications include many books and articles on musical subjects, the most recent being *Women in Music: A Research and Information Guide* (Routledge, 2010).

Born in Rochester, Minnesota, **Frank Pendle** holds Master's and PhD degrees in American history from Kent State University. He has taught at universities in Canada and the United States, including the University of Cincinnati. He is also an enthusiastic performer of choral music, and was a member of Cincinnati's May Festival Chorus for over fifteen years. He is currently retired.

Catherine Roma, Professor of Music at Wilmington College, is first and foremost an active choral director in the greater Cincinnati area. Her 2008 Governor's Arts Award, for community development and participation, reflects her devotion and engagement in the choral arts. Roma is founder and director of MUSE, Cincinnati's Women's Choir, a nationally recognized community arts organization dedicated to musical excellence and social change. She is co-founder and co-director of the Martin Luther King Chorale, an interracial, inter-denominational, inter-generational, city-wide choir. The King Chorale provided the core of the 700-voice chorus organized to sing at the ground breaking for the National Underground Railroad Freedom Center in Cincinnati in 2002 and its grand opening in 2004. Roma also serves as Minister of Music at St. John's Unitarian Universalist Church. Through her association with Wilmington College, Roma started UMOJA Men's Chorus in 1993 at Warren Correctional Institution at the request of the Dean of Correctional Education at Wilmington College. She believes choral communities inspire, motivate, educate, and heal an ailing world.

INDEX

Music Hall and Union Terminal
dominate this photo collage of
images from Cincinnati's Over-
the-Rhine and West End.